The History

During ancient times, people faced many challenges while gardening. Being the curious animal man is, he wanted to find out what really made plants grow. Soil was a mysterious material that somehow provided the right conditions for greenery to grow from seed into plants that produced edible parts. Often plagues and pestilences reduced or even destroyed the yields of plants that societies heavily depended on for their well-being. When crops failed, societies suffered famine and death. Such crop failures led to wars between neighboring communities and even the death of entire civilizations and cultures.

I heard the phrase "No Agriculture, No Culture" recently on a TV historical documentary. This statement points out the fact that cultures and civilizations are dependent on crops for their survival. This became the basis of agriculture to find out the reasons for plants to thrive so that man could cultivate plants under favorable conditions, which would lead to abundant production. Ancient civilizations became aware that water was essential for any agricultural practice, so populations gathered in areas that had an abundant source of water that could be used for growing plants. Usually, by streams, rivers, lakes, or springs that had fresh water, civilizations developed where they easily could practice agriculture. Fertile soil existed in valleys of rivers and near lakes. Such soil supported productive crops and human centers. When groups of inhabitants experienced harsh environments that restricted their crops, they needed to examine what factors reduced yields and what could be done to improve them.

In the early times, man became aware of growing plants in specific environments and tried new methods of cultivation.

Egyptian hieroglyphic records of several hundred years BC describe growing plants in water. According to historical sources, Theophrastus during 372–287 BC experimented for the first time with plant nutrition. A form of hydroponics was established in the hanging gardens of Babylon, the floating gardens of the Aztecs of Mexico, and the Chinese. However, these were not called "hydroponic" culture even though they were a form of it. Further experiments with a scientific approach to discovering plant constituents were carried out by numerous scientists during the 17th century and later, they

were able to discover that water, soil, and air provided elements such as carbon, hydrogen, and oxygen that were constituents of plant matter.

Researchers later continued to demonstrate that the minerals that plants contained came From the soil via the soil Water. This enabled scientists to later grow plants in water alone without soil provided that these minerals were added to the water. This became "nutriculture" where plant roots were immersed in a water solution containing salts of their essential elements. From 1925 to 1935, laboratory-scale nutriculture was expanded to commercial-scale production of crops. However, it was not until the 1930s and 1940s that the application of nutriculture was applied on a commercial scale by Dr. W. F. Gericke of the University of California and termed "hydroponics". The word "hydroponics" was derived from two Greek words hydro ("water") and ponos ("labor")—"water working" In the 1940s, with the war in the Pacific, Gericke applied hydroponics to commercial production in the non-arable islands where troops were stationed.

After the war, hydroponic culture was adopted by the greenhouse industry to resolve problems with soil-borne diseases and pests as well as structural and nutritional challenges faced by year-round growing in greenhouses. Now, almost all crops are grown in greenhouses, including vegetables and ornamentals, use some form of hydroponics. It may also be termed "soil-less culture" when using an inert medium other than soil to which a nutrient solution is added.

Hydroponics VS. Traditional Soil

Advantages of Hydroponics

There is more than one difference between them, and in this chapter, we're going to go over the differences between developing flora hydroponically or in soil indoors; how a good deal the yield, how taste and aroma are affected and how everyday plant growth differs.

Space Savings

Hydroponics saves a gorgeous amount of space compared to usual soil gardening. Usually, a plant's roots want an area to spread out via the soil. Not anymore! Instead, they are submerged in a bath of oxygenated nutrient solution. Instead of the usage of soil as a service for the nutrients your crops need, hydroponics makes use of a personalized nutrient answer to surround your plants with flawlessly calibrated vitamins all of the time.

Because of this, you get to pack your vegetation nearer together, ensuing in a huge area savings!

Hydroponics Saves Water

Let's suppose about how the common soil gardener waters their plants. Usually every few days they dump an exact amount of water into their soil, making sure correct penetration into the soil so the roots can suck it up. Some of that water drips out of the bottom of their container or seeps also into the ground. Some of it evaporates out of the soil.

Only a small proportion of the water is used by using the plant. Hydroponics solves this trouble with the aid of using what is referred to as a recirculating nutrient reservoir in most kinds of systems (Deep Water Culture is one of the most popular). This means that a plant's roots will only take up the amount of water they need at any one time and depart the rest in the reservoir for later. The reservoir is blanketed to prevent evaporation and no water can seep out of the bottom. This approves the same quantity of water that was used to water a plant in soil for a day to water a plant in a hydroponics set up for days or weeks at a time. You can retailer round 90% of the water used in soil gardening definitely with the aid of switching to a hydroponic setup.

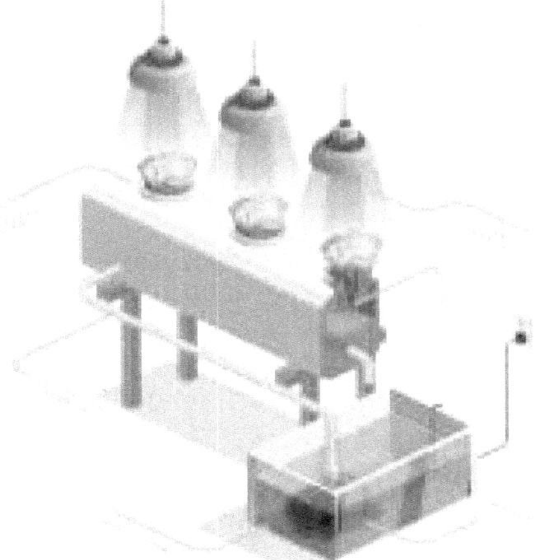

No Weeding Necessary

One of the most common excuses I hear when anybody tells me why they don't desire to garden is:

"I don't want to spend all of my time on my palms and knees weeding!"

Easy solution. Switch to hydroponics. No soil, no weeds. Everything's neater.

Less Pests and Diseases - Hydroponic Pests

No Soil = No More of These Bad Boys

Following that identical logic, pests and illnesses are appreciably decreased in hydroponics. Soil is taken out of the picture and changed with one of the common hydroponic growing media. Eliminating soil additionally eliminates a lot of the specific soil-borne diseases and pests that plague usual gardening.

Time Savings

This is my favorite cause of all. Not only does developing hydroponically save you the time of weeding, pest control, and watering, it also speeds up the growth of the plant.

If you're growing outdoors, that means you get to squeeze in more harvest cycles before your developing season ends. You also get to observe the growth of plant life at a faster pace and study about all of the unique things you could do to improve the boom a whole lot quicker.

For example, you can take ahead of lettuce from seedling to harvest in around a month in hydroponics compared to two months in soil. Imagine how a good deal faster you could come to be a gardening professional with a time financial savings like that!

Gives You Extreme Control!

All of the motives above combine to form one powerful motive why hydroponics (and all soil-less growing, for that matter) dominates soil gardening: control.

You become the grasp of your plant's environment. It's up to you to create the best nutrient mixture, temperature, humidity, and growing schedule. It's a form of like that film "The Truman Show". You're the showrunner, and your flora is Truman. You flip the solar on and off. You control when your flowers get fed and what they eat. You're responsible for their well-being. It's a terrific thing!

Hydroponics VS. Aeroponic

Aeroponics is an indoor gardening exercise in which flowers are grown and nourished by suspending their root structures in air and usually spraying them with a nutrient and water solution.

Soil is now not used for aeroponics because the flowers can thrive when their roots are constantly or periodically uncovered to a nutrient-rich mist.

Aeroponics affords an efficient skill to grow plants, including fruits and vegetables, except potting and repotting them to top off their access to nutrient-rich soil.

The National Aeronautics and Space Administration (NASA) examined the effectiveness of aeroponics on the Mir area station and the results showed that Asian bean seedlings should develop effectively in a nutrient solution in zero gravity.

Plants are suspended in the air in enclosed frames that leave the leafy suggestions and the roots able to grow up and down respectively. Many aeroponic structures seem very similar to common potted plant systems, with the key difference being that the containers for the flowers are sealed around the plants' bases and have a closed environment for the root systems.

Instead of relying on a combination of soil and water to feed the plants, aeroponic horticulturists spray the root systems with a nutrient mix. Because the roots are enclosed, the nutrient-water combine is used more efficiently via the plants and less water is needed for them to grow and thrive.

With aeroponics, indoor horticulturists may also use vertical and horizontal houses to develop greater plants using less flooring area and they preserve water by using sealed aeroponic systems.

Depending on the aeroponic system, nutrients may be sprayed manually at intervals at some stage in the day and night, but most aeroponic systems have one or extra pumps that automatically hold plants nourished except steady supervision. As long as the device is sealed and nutrient mist is constantly pumped to the roots, flowers need to thrive in an aeroponic environment.

Aeroponic systems nourish plants with nothing greater than nutrient-laden mist. The thought builds off that of hydroponic systems, in which the roots are held in a soilless developing medium, such as coco coir, over which nutrient-laden water is periodically pumped. Aeroponics genuinely dispenses with the developing medium, leaving the roots to dangle in the air, where they are periodically puffed by using specially-designed misting devices.

In aeroponics systems, seeds are "planted" in portions of foam stuffed into tiny pots, which are exposed to light on one end and nutrient mist on the other. The foam additionally holds the stem and root mass in location as the vegetation grows.

The Advantages of Aeroponics

Who knew naked roots might survive, abundant less thrive? It turns out that eliminating the growing medium is very liberating for a plants' roots: the greater oxygen they are uncovered to results in quicker growth. Aeroponic structures are also extremely water-efficient. These closed-loop structures use 95 percent much less irrigation than flowers grown in soil. And because the vitamins are held in the water, they get recycled, too.

In addition to these efficiencies, aeroponics' eco-friendly reputation is bolstered by the ability to grow large portions of meals in small spaces. The strategy is employed in indoor vertical farms, which are increasingly common in cities – reducing down on the environmental expenses of getting food from area to plate. And because aeroponics structures are fully enclosed, there is no nutrient runoff to foul close by waterways. Rather than treating pests and disease with harsh chemicals, the growing gear has to be sterilized as needed.

Major difference between hydroponics and aeroponics

In a hydroponic system, plants are grown without soil. They are instead grown with added nutrients in sand, liquid or gravel. Aeroponics is a form of hydroponics, and it uses no growing medium. This is because as already stated, crops do not require soil to grow; the soil actually can hinder the plant's growth.

Since all plants need nutrients, the plant expends valuable energy growing and stretching their roots to find these nutrients for flower formulation and growth. In both the hydroponic and aeroponic systems, these nutrients are delivered straight to the plants' roots.

Hydroponics Growing Medium

With the hydroponic system, crops are placed in a growing medium, such as perlite, clay pebbles or coconut husks. A nutrient-rich solution then flows through the airy planting medium providing food for crop growth.

Growing Medium With Aeroponics

The aeroponics system doesn't require or use any growing medium. Crops are suspended in a dark enclosure, while the nutrient-dense solution is sprayed on the roots at set certain intervals. Aeroponic system is a type of hydroponic system.

TYPES OF HYDROPONIC SYSTEMS

A   lthough there is a great deal of variety in the different types of hydroponic systems, in essence, it comes down to six different types. The drip system, the ebb and flow system, N.F.T., the water culture system, aeroponics, and the wick system. These systems can all be modified to suit the environment and budget of the individual user and the space they have available to them. In choosing an appropriate system for your own needs you need to consider these things as well as the size and types of plant you will be growing. Remember also that systems will need to cleaned thoroughly from time to time so look for a unit that you can disassemble and clean easily.

The Drip System

This is one of the most popular systems both for the home gardener and the commercial producer. One of the main reasons that it is so popular is that it facilitates the production of large plants. Each plant is potted into a growing medium in an individual pot. A drip line is then extended from the reservoir to each pot and when the pump is turned on nutrient solution drips into the pots until the medium is soaked through. The excess solution then drains through the pot to where it is captured in a tray which returns it to the reservoir using gravity. The timer is set to turn the pump on again just before the medium gets dry so that the roots are kept constantly moist.

In domestic units, these systems tend to be circulating but some commercial units are non- circulating. What happens in these larger operations is that when the water drains through the growing medium it is not captured. This may sound wasteful but it relies on the fact that the timer is so accurate that when set correctly it gives enough solution to the growing medium to wet it exactly with very little waste. Just before the medium dries it then adds more solution. The advantage to the commercial grower is twofold. Firstly, he is not required to have a huge area of catchment trays running the solution back to the reservoir and secondly each time he tops up the reservoir he can replace the exact amount of nutrient appropriate to the plants' needs. The nutrients within a system decrease as they are absorbed by the plant and so a circulating system must be checked frequently to measure the nutrient levels.

In a non-circulating system, the reservoir must be topped up frequently but on large scale operations, there are normally staff in place to see to this.

Ebb & Flow System

This is a method that suits the smaller scale of the domestic user either in the house or in the garden because it is easy to build and can be designed to fit into any available space. Plants are potted into a growing medium and placed into a fairly deep tray. An overflow line is connected to the tray at a level of one or two inches below the surface of the growing medium and water is then pumped from the reservoir into the tray. When the water level reaches the overflow it simply runs back to the reservoir. When this starts a float valve turns off the pump. The same valve turns the water back on again when the reservoir refills. In this way, the roots of the plant are constantly being submerged in a solution and drained again. It is a system that can be made on a tiny scale and many pre-made systems utilize this method. When building your system be sure that the overflow pipe is sufficiently large to carry away water faster than it can arrive via the pump.

Nutrient Film Technique

In this system, plants are grown in a matt of material such as rock wool and placed into a tray with a fine film at its base. A pump carries the nutrients through the film and this soaks the film keeping the roots constantly damp. Excess water simply runs back to the reservoir via gravity. Plants are normally planted through some sort of material to keep light from reaching the roots as there is no growing medium to cover them.

The system can be very small but when used on large scale operations long channels are filled with film and the same system is just notched up to a greater size. Because of the shallow depth of this system, it is most suited to small fast-growing crops such as lettuce and certain types of herb. The system is very effective but with small fast-growing plants of this nature, there is a risk of them dying quickly in the event of the roots drying out so there is little time to respond if there is some sort of breakdown in the system such as electrical failure.

Water Culture System

In this system, the root is constantly kept wet by the very fine splashing of tiny droplets of nutrient mix. The plants are suspended with their roots hanging down into the reservoir. Instead of a water pump, an air pump is placed into the reservoir and the water aerated at a pressure that will make the water look like it is boiling lightly. Because the top of the roots is just above the nutrient mix level the bubbling effect created by the pump will cause droplets to hit the roots. This system can be as simple as a large plastic bucket with a hole or holes cut into the lid through which the roots are suspended. The air pump is then placed in the bottom of the bucket and the lid put back on. (You may need to cut a groove for the lead to the pump). The most difficult part of the operation is setting the water depth so that it adequately splashes the roots. Don't worry if the lower roots touch the solution as long as there is still plenty of root material exposed to the air. Make sure that the lid is made of a material that will keep the roots in the dark. This method ensures a well-oxygenated mix reaching the roots but it also requires monitoring of the depth of the solution. More sophisticated systems of the water culture system are used commercially but at the same time, it is just an upgrade of the system used by the Aztecs that I mentioned at the beginning of this book.

Aeroponics System

Another variation of the hydroponic system is called aeroponics but as you will see the main principals differ very little from the other techniques you have seen so far. Once again the plants are supported above the solution supply only this time the solution is mist sprayed onto the roots. Like with NFT, no growing medium is needed. Think of those small fine sprays you have on an ordinary garden irrigation system. The nutrient solution is pumped from the reservoir and instead of going directly to the routes, it passes through the sprayers which wet the roots with a fine mist of water. Excess water can then be captured in trays and run back to the reservoir although the spray spreads the water further and so recapturing the nutrient solution is harder. Most commercial units don't attempt to recapture the moisture but instead, try to regulate the delivery system so precisely that there is minimal waste.

The Wick System

Of all the systems that have been discussed so far, this is by far the simplest one. The plants being grown are potted in their growing medium and then suspended above a bucket of nutrient mix. At its most basic you could have a plastic container with a plant inside balanced on a bucket of nutrients. A wicking material is then placed between the growing medium and the nutrient mix. This can be any material that will carry moisture such as a hemp rope, strips of carpet under-felt or some twisted strips of hessian sacking. There are no moving parts, material costs are minimal if any, and there is very little skill needed to put it all together.

There are anyway numerous issues with this strategy. First and foremost just little plans ought to be developed as the wick, regardless of whether you utilize a few, can not convey adequate water to fulfill the requirements of a bigger plant. Furthermore, the wick won't move the supplements uniformly and those left behind in the repository will move toward structure a buildup that could become poisonous to the plant. Thirdly there is no oxygenation occurring in the repository. This implies could be utilized by a novice to grow a couple of little plants as a prologue to different frameworks of aquaculture. It is additionally frequently involved by educators as a method to

exhibit fine activity as that is the thing is occurring here. Certain individuals utilize a L formed cylinder to convey water to the lower part of a plants roots. Whenever the water is poured down the line it will be conveyed upwards by hairlike activity in the developing medium however this isn't aquaculture in its actual sense as conceived by Dr. William Gerricke.

NOT AQUAPONICS!

There is one more framework called hydroponics which is frequently mistaken for tank-farming and has numerous likenesses however it isn't viewed as obvious aquaculture. Hydroponics chiefs include utilizing the waste matter made by fish to take care of plants with a framework basically the same as those of aquaculture. Adding supplements in controlled amounts is so vital for the way of thinking behind aquaculture that the two subjects are best considered separately.

Choosing Your Hydroponic System

Choosing which aqua-farming framework to introduce in your home expects you to consider numerous factors and to conclude which makes the biggest difference to you. Among them are accessible space, mechanization, energy necessities, crop determination, favored area of the tank-farming nursery, support requests, usability, and how much support and upkeep each requires. Starting expense is significant as well, obviously, just like the expense for energy utilization, inputs, and other continuous support expenses.

Available space

You need to, as a matter of first importance, check your developing page to choose the available space. This is on the grounds that the space available decides the quantity of pots or cans that can be covered in a given tank-farming framework. This will at last choose the quantity of plants that you can fill in your creating site.

In many cases, the more modest aqua-farming frameworks expect around sixteen rectangular ft of deck space. You should furthermore assemble a more prominent region that will be utilized to keep the water repository, lighting, siphon, and coolers. In this way, examining your creating site close by space is a key necessity.

Automation

Hydroponics frameworks have additional elements like siphons, develop lights, and coolers which are necessary in guaranteeing the best stages are accomplished while creating plants. On the lookout, there are both robotized and guide designs and it's the obligation of the grounds-keeper to pick the great framework that ensures efficiency.

Recent examination has demonstrated that most indoor cultivating disappointment happens because of terrible temperature management.

Purchasing a programmed framework will give you a simple time while creating vegetation on the grounds that the situation will naturally control the required most attractive levels.

The advanced constructions have electronic units that consequently uncover moistness, temperature, lighting, and water goes along these lines, alleviating you a ton of

manual change burden.

Expandability of the Hydroponics System

As an amateur, you would perhaps need to take a stab at planting with a little tank-farming gadget pack and later increment it to foster more plants. Whenever you are happy with the upsides of preparing this helpful and agreeable cultivating technique, you can organize to stretch out the framework to keep more noteworthy plants.

For this situation, you want to have sufficient room that can hold additional pails or pots to accurately oblige the additional plants. Expandability of the device decides your complete result and something basic can assist you with making the legitimate choice.

Energy efficiency

Every tank-farming machine is worked the utilization of electrical energy that helps siphoning, lighting, and cooling. Power charges can run high particularly when a rancher declines to utilize energy-saving LED bulbs. A full range of gentle is wished during the gadget to guarantee top-quality development of your plants.

Therefore, while purchasing your aquaculture framework, typically verify that you use energy-saving LED bulbs and this will go an extended way in limiting your working expenses.

System charge and setup costs

Hydroponics constructions can be sold as pre-fabricated or the grounds-keeper can decide to gather one. Building your own DIY Hydroponics gadget at home will require proficient transporter the spot you should lease an expert to set the framework set up on the off chance that you can't do so.

This would potentially be costly to fledglings and it requires shut management meaning you should be there over installation.

On the other hand, the market has a huge exhibit of pre-fabricated aquaculture frameworks that are modified to bathing suit your inclination. With the entire parcel previously set up, you will exclusively be expected to set the framework in your ideal area and launch your indoor cultivating task appropriately away.

Choosing a System by Crop

Knowing what you need to develop ought to be the principal thought while picking an aquaculture framework. A few frameworks can grow a wide scope of yields (i.e., flood and channel) and a few frameworks turn out best for crops with explicit development propensities. One of the principal frameworks in this section is an aquaculture bottle garden. This framework turns out incredible for verdant green yields like lettuce and basil however is awful for bigger harvests like tomatoes. You ought to likewise consider the variety of harvests you need to develop. Would you like to develop crops with a wide scope of supplement prerequisites and wanted pH ranges? The most ideal choice some of the time is to have numerous frameworks. The most outstanding aspect of developing plants is that they are by and large simple to supplant! Try different things with new yields and gain for a fact. I offer a ton of rules in this part and helpful yield determination notes in the reference section, yet these rules are not intended to keep you from testing. Many yields will fill in conditions outside of their optimal reach. Plants are definitely more open minded than we give them credit for. Don't hesitate for even a moment to attempt; there are generally more seeds to plant!

Choosing a System by Location

There are tank-farming frameworks for developing lettuce in space! Regardless of your area, there is potential to develop plants hydroponically. I even have an aquaculture garden in my RV. For every one of the frameworks recorded in this part, I give area ideas. A significant number of these frameworks can be changed for inside, outside, little spaces, or huge ones.

Choosing a System by Maintenance Requirements

The proportion of plants to the volume of water is by and large the greatest variable for assessing support necessities. A framework with a little supply and a ton of plants will require incessant support on the grounds that the cultivator should add water and alter the repository with compost as the plants rapidly lessen the water level in the repository. Frameworks with a high plant-to-water proportion likewise will quite often gather an imbalanced proportion of supplements and require successive full framework flushes. Another element that will impact the support necessity is crop determination. Crops like tomatoes, peppers, and cucumbers might require trellising and pruning relying upon the assortment. A few yields become rapidly and should be supplanted frequently, as microgreens, and they'll require a great deal of work since they should be cultivated and reaped weekly.

Choosing a System by Difficulty

Although I could never prevent somebody from beginning with a high level aqua-farming framework, I am mindful that numerous grounds-keepers need to prevail from the beginning. Hard to-utilize frameworks might have an expectation to absorb information. I love learning! You could as well. But you also might value simplicity and using a hydroponic system that has minimal moving parts and few opportunities for failure.

Some frameworks are incredible novice amicable frameworks that don't need power. Flood and Drain is one of the very fledgling amicable frameworks, notwithstanding, it makes them move parts that require power. Dribble, Nutrient Film Technique, and Aeroponics are not as simple to set up and are a piece troublesome, so they probably won't be the most ideal choice for a first-time frame aqua-farming rancher. Be that as it may, the alleged trouble level of a framework shouldn't put you off attempting the framework assuming it meets your requirements. The trouble of utilizing a framework is absolutely a conviction and you could discover a portion of the less amateur amicable frameworks the simplest to use!

BASIC PARTS OF A HYDROPONIC GROWING SYSTEM

Hydroponic systems vary, but they also have major similar components. These constitute what is required for the system to be complete and function as required to prevent failures. You may choose to work with the generally given units on the lookout or decide to build one as a person. Whichever decision you go for, there are a few essential parts that everybody will require. This will incorporate a developing media, develop lights supplies, as well as a supplement arrangement. Also, you should consider the customary maintenance.

Grow Light

Indoor plant development requires lighting that intently looks like that of the sun. In this, you really want a full range of light. In this, there are various kinds of light arrangements relying upon the plants you need to develop. Glaring lights are great for developing foliage plants as they supplement normal lighting notwithstanding not having the option to give a full spectrum.

On the other hand, blooming plants and vegetables will require better lighting and hence the utilization of metal halide lights. These are intended to give the nearest similitudes to daylight. High-pressure sodium lights are likewise a thought and it is critical to take note of that these give more red/orange range. These are significant for the course of photosynthesis and chlorophyll creation. You can incorporate light movers or potentially reflectors to assist with supporting the effectiveness of lighting.

Growing Medium

A developing medium replaces soil in normal development. There are different developing mediums and relying upon the kind of aqua-farming; you will actually want to pick the best medium to work with. Developing mediums hold every one of the supplements that you would require for growth.

The most well-known mediums utilized incorporate Rockwool and extended mud as they give more benefits when contrasted with different mediums. Notwithstanding, it isn't restricting to only these two and others might utilize sand, rock, bark, coconut fiber, vermiculite, polyurethane froth, as well as perlite.

Rockwool enjoys the additional benefit of holding more water content while simultaneously supporting air course with the roots.

Expanded dirt enjoys the additional benefit of advancing air flow. Plus, it is pH impartial and after some time, it won't minimal making it durable.

Nutrient Solution

The supplement arrangement is likely the main piece of a tank-farming framework. It could sound complex, yet it's simply an extravagant approach to saying supplements broke up in water! The supplement arrangement is liable for holding every one of the essential supplements expected by your plants. The arrangement is just water and the supplements which will be held by a repository. The arrangement ought to be water-dissolvable with negligible buildup. Far and away superior, an answer with no buildup is fitting as this won't lessen support prerequisites. Additionally, guarantee that you change the arrangement as required running somewhere in the range of one and two weeks.

Going for an aqua-farming supplement arrangement is suggested as it has the expected extents of the important supplements. Additionally, it evades a poisonous level for your plants. Before you can make due with a supplement arrangement, you ought to test its electrical conductivity level. This is finished with the assistance of a conductivity meter. Remember that a high electrical conductivity means a vegetative development instead of blossoms and fruits.

The sum will fluctuate with the thought of different factors, for example, the quantity of plants and the age of the plants as more youthful plants will consume

less. Different elements will be resolved in view of the kind of hydroponics.

Nutrient Reservoir

This is in the same place as the arrangement put for use before the plants get sufficiently close to it. It isn't limiting to what you can use as a supplement repository. One can utilize an old fish tank, a huge plastic compartment or any hardware that can hold the amount of water you need.

However, while you can look over changed materials, you ought to stay away from repositories produced using metallic materials. This is on the grounds that they are probably going to present different parts that are thought of as unsafe to the plants. Solid plastic is enthusiastically prescribed as it is likewise simple to clean and keep up with for right about anybody even a fledgling in hydroponics.

Grow Tray

A develop plate effectively holds the plants. Many think that the plants are set in the supplement arrangement however this isn't true. Plants are isolated. The plants are filled in the develop plate for sure is generally alluded to as the develop chamber. Others will utilize pots, particularly for limited scope development. This will change additionally relying upon the kind of tank-farming. A provider will direct you through the advantages and difficulties of utilizing one develop plate instead of another.

Pump

A siphon effectively pumps water from the supply. Its key object is to oxygenate the water and forestall green growth development in the supply. This is like that of an aquarium. The flow makes it simpler to guarantee that the water is new and clean. Each aquaculture framework should incorporate a siphon. Guarantee that it doesn't impede as this will adversely influence the plants. Continually mind its usefulness to forestall any blockages.

Airstone

An airstone is typically included however it's anything but a fundamental need. It is energetically suggested as it effectively adds oxygen into the supplement arrangement. Oxygen is required even for traditional cultivation to help facilitate germination and overall healthy growth. More oxygen creation implies that you will support quicker development as well as keep the supplement arrangement new for use.

Delivery System

Most of aquaculture frameworks keep the develop plate separate from the supplement repository. The plants need to get to the supplement arrangement, and it is the occupation of the conveyance framework to take care of the plants. The conveyance framework is liable for moving the supplement arrangement from the supplement repository to the develop plate and afterward depleting the overabundance arrangement back into the reservoir.

Grow Tents

Grow tents give an encased space to natural controls, lights, and developing frameworks. Now and then it very well may be challenging to establish the appropriate developing environment inside, or the ideal developing environment may not be a similar environment you wish to have in the remainder of your indoor space. Plants might like stickiness proportions around 50 to 80 percent, yet individuals frequently really like to be in mugginess outside of that reach. Develop tents are an extraordinary method for disconnecting the plants in an indoor climate. Other than keeping a different environment from the remainder of the indoor space, a develop tent can keep in the splendid light expected for plant growth.

Intake Fans

An admission fan put outwardly can save significant development space in the develop tent. In this arrangement, the air is driven into the develop tent and the exhaust inactively escapes from ducting ports. This positive strain develop room is extraordinary for bug the executives on the grounds that the debilitating air makes it challenging for irritations to get into the develop tent. A negative tension develop tent can now and then suck in bothers close to any potential openings, however a positive strain develop tent will make an outward wind current that makes it challenging for irritations to enter the develop tent from anyplace yet the admission fan. There are some hard core air admission channels, similar to the HEPA channel displayed at left, that can forestall bugs, microbes, organisms, and dust from entering a develop room.

Grow lights can produce a ton of hotness and it could be challenging to deal with that hotness with just ventilation fans. Cooling units devoted exclusively to the develop room are at times vital for indoor grounds-keepers utilizing exceptionally strong lights, utilizing numerous lights, filling in warm environments, or developing temperature-delicate crops.

PLANNING YOUR GARDEN

How To Set-up Your Own Hydroponic Garden

By definition, growing hydroponically potential a grower isn't the use of soil as a growing medium. The word hydroponics comes from Latin and potential working water. The intent and scope of this chapter is not to outfit a succinct and entire arrangement of instructions

for growing hydroponically, be that as it may, to give a customary outline of the very a few stages and approaches so novice landscapers have a higher reasoning of what may moreover be involved.

As usual, do an exhaustive query on every one of the different components yourself to boost your peril for progress. Everything cultivating can concede undesired outcomes and outings will strikingly expand your chances.

Deepwater culture aquaculture advancement utilizes no medium not quite the same as water for feeding the roots. Thus, with this methodology, keeping the water circling and amazing circulated air through is basic to establish endurance. Supplement stages should furthermore be held firmly at the OK levels for plant life, and there is no genuine space for disregarding the essentials. You can't simply walk away from this kind of contraption for some days.

This technique, albeit certainly truly outstanding for plant yields, may likewise now not be for the amateur. On the different hand, tank-farming frameworks that utilization a developing medium other than water have a truckload additional wiggle room yet addresses an eminent area to start creating hydroponically.

Expanded dirt, Rockwool, perlite, sand or rock are famous foster modes for aquaculture developing. The crucial qualification between utilizing these mediums and soil is that dirt will by and large keep up with dampness parcels longer than the others. Allowing roots to dry out throughout the customary blast cycle is a certain method for losing them.

For this part, I will involve further developed earth for instance. These are the little round bundles of fire, normally going on dirt. They are pH unbiased, reusable and don't conservative. Thus, they keep up with the indistinguishable dampness maintenance boundaries after some time. They really do dry out incredibly quick, so you'll should be cautious while picking your watering time.

Perlite has a few likenesses to dirt pellets anyway because of a few of the particles are very minuscule (earth pellets ar amazingly uniform in size), perlite can stop up producers. There are a few other central issues for a tank-farming framework the use of broadened mud, which are:

There is compelling reason need to discard the old media (as is every once in a while wished with soil), so the drawn out charge is diminished, as is the issue of disposing of the antiquated media)

It is lightweight, so it is less convoluted to move enormous pots.

It's various, minuscule air pockets outfit an exact wellspring of oxygen and help keep up with moisture.

Preparation Of The Grow Media

With further developed dirt (likewise with numerous other made media), you'll like to wash and sanitize it sooner than use. You'll want to do this initially and with each re-use. In the event that it's not useful to utilize the develop pots for washing the pellets, observe a monstrous compartment that without issues permits flushing and draining.

You'll need to be exhaustive to get every one of the past roots and noteworthy nutrients off while re-utilizing the pellets. At first, there is only some purifying of soil and prudent sanitizing to do. Water is the top notch for cleaning, essentially continue to wash. Top notch water is higher than endeavoring to utilize some cleaner that your vegetation won't regard later.

Disinfecting can be executed by weakened dye or hydrogen peroxide. Weaken fade to 10% and hydrogen peroxide to 3%. Sterilization forestalls contrary to minute irritations in your nursery, which don't unquestionably have numerous normal hunters when they taint the framework, so trying to see there are essentially as not many as achievable before you start will be appropriately rewarded.

Let the sanitizer stand on the media for at least on hour. Make sure to entirely wash off any such sanitizer sooner than beginning. Shape can be an additional a provoking vermin to take out. Whenever it is distinguished, changing the pellets is regularly basic.

Planting And Growing Tips For Hydroponics

Beginning plants from seeds is a subject for some articles and portraying how to do so would conceivably remove the focal point of basically looking at a solitary sort of aqua-farming framework. Presumably the best strategy I will know about is to utilize a Rockwool develop 3D shape and hatch it in a damp climate. The water utilized for new roots should be as liberated from chlorine (or any various poisons) as could be expected. Utilizing RO or refined waterworks, or you can de-chlorinate the water yourself.

If you are relocating from a dirt pot, you will want to delicately discard the dirt from around the roots and wash with top notch water. Try not to leave soil on the foundations of a plant as this might cause microorganisms or fungous pervasion and plant disease.

Soil additionally will connect producers a really recycled watering framework. Make a cone-molded dampened pellet area where you lay the completely soaked roots and cowl them with wet dirt pellets. Start watering right away. Try not to allow new verdure to have a dry cycle by any stretch of the imagination until they have introduced for somewhere around seven to 10 days.

When transplantation to the new pot, do in this way as though establishing clean root. It is advantageous to Use a little net pot. Place pellets in the base, lay your root contraption over them and add pellets to the highest point of the root system.

When relocated, the new root foundation is little and the water applied to the pellets needs to dampen the pellets the spot the roots are. Involving a net pot for these roots, and seeing that there are two or three sluggish trickles directly around here, will help.

If you are relocating from a foster 3D shape, the region the block neck-somewhere down in the earth media in a net pot, and afterward relocate the web pot into your regular dirt pellet pot.

When inundating the little net pot into your foster pot, put you form pot into an enormous container loaded down with water. The pellets will be overall suspended, making it much less muddled to embed the net pot into the media at the right profundity, which will be base of the plant-don't submerse the plant! In this model, there are no dirt particles to put off before transplanting.

Nutrition Tips For Hydroponics

When vegetation is more youthful and presently relocated, high-nitrogen manure will animate the plant in the incorrect manner. Nitrogen produces foliar increment and new greenery needs to initially foster more prominent roots. Thus, the supplement strategy you'll need to utilize will trade as your vegetation mature. Frequently in soil, there as of now exists an enormous amount of full scale and micronutrients, however in tank-farming, soilless cultivating there by and large aren't any aside from you add them. Once more, this component is never again advanced science, however it requires some comprehension of what vegetation needs and what excellent composts to supply to create sound, enthusiastically creating plants.

Choosing The Right Medium For Your Hydroponic System

In aqua-farming, a "developing medium" is what you will use in the district of soil to area your plants' foundations. While fostering your aquaculture framework, it is basic that you select a medium that meets your requirements, will supply you the biggest yields, and will be the least demanding to keep up with. The following are a couple of the most well known creating media utilized in current tank-farming frameworks, and the endowments and negative parts of each.

Rockwool

Rockwool is conceivably the most famous creating medium utilized in contemporary aquaculture frameworks. It is a texture produced using basalt rock and which, which is liquefied and "turned" so the material transforms into interconnected filaments. One of the essential benefits of Rockwool is that it holds water quite well, which limit that your vegetation are less likely to be hurt through lack of hydration assuming your siphon fizzles. It likewise holds a wonderful arrangement of air, which capacity that it will make it more noteworthy not going for your greenery to be over watered. Nonetheless, the residue and filaments from this developing medium can be dangerous, so you need to cautious when you manage it. Since this fabric has an exorbitant pH level, you could likewise need to pay elite interest to the pH phase of your supplement reply to ensure the plants in your

aquaculture machine stay healthy.

Coconut Fiber

Coconut fiber, now and again known as coco coir, is, in all actuality, the powdered husks of coconuts. It is filling in acknowledgment because of the reality it is one of the natural media accessible for aqua-farming frameworks. It is perceived for its huge oxygen and water limit, which potential your vegetation has a higher peril of getting by assuming something turns out badly with your aquaculture framework. In any case, some less expensive coconut fiber is recognized to join gigantic measures of ocean salt, which can likewise hurt your crop.

Perlite

Perlite could be a sort of volcanic stone. Perlite is one of the more low evaluated media you can find and is routinely mixed with various media. In light of its cost and great wicking activity, this is the media ordinarily viewed as in less expensive wick aquaculture frameworks. Nonetheless, it doesn't stand any kind of test quite well, and on the grounds that it tends to be perilous whenever ingested, you should also utilize a residue cover when handling.

Expanded Clay Pebbles

Clay rocks are for all intents and purposes made via baking earth in a furnace, fostering a lot of air-filled dirt pellets. Extended mud pellets are one of the extra expensive media you can use in your aquaculture framework, yet they may also obviously retailer you a touch of money over the long haul on the grounds that not at all like most unique developing media, they are reusable. Nonetheless, earth stones in all actuality do never again hold water or oxygen quite well, and accordingly may expect you to blend them in with another medium to expand water retention.

Air

Using air as a medium, which is additionally infrequently alluded to as utilizing "no medium," is exceptionally cost-accommodating, on the grounds that it in the event that honestly limit that you don't need to purchase a medium. Since your foundations are continually uncovered to air, you can moreover persistently be ensured that they are ceaselessly getting the oxygen that they need. Remember, notwithstanding, that involving air as the medium in your aquaculture gadget pretty much rules out blunder. On the off chance that your siphon fizzles, your underlying foundations can dry out in a count number of minutes, fundamentally inconvenient or even rapidly killing your total crop.

Determining The Correct Watering Cycle For Your Plants

Is your gadget lazy trickle or quick? You will need a huge siphon and utilize greater power for a speedy dribble. These producers will ordinarily take care of for 5 to 10 mph (gallons each hour) each, thus in all actuality do never again have the assets for as beneficial conveyance of water as a lazy 0.5-to 1.0-mph emitter.

Because expanded earth pellets will dry out amazingly quick, do never again have the watering embarked for a really long time a length of time. Abstain from creating in regions uncovered to moving dry air; this will intention the pellets to dry out prematurely.

Test your watering cycle out prior to getting begun with plants. Famous watering cycles use on/off occurrences of 15 minutes and onwards. Attempt to avoid an off length of extra than 30 minutes. Assuming the utilization of a languid dribble framework, you can set extensive watering times (say five hours or more) with 15-to 30-minute off intervals.

Slow trickle siphons eat little power. The off cycles can draw out the presence of the siphon. A 250-gph siphon is fruitful in water up to 50 plants the spot the dribble charge sums 1 gph per plant. This cost is normal. The clock you select will have a huge bearing on your watering cycle.

You'll lean toward a water utility framework that makes a top showing of appropriating the water over the outer layer of the media. Just a trickle or two is done going to do effectively. In a perfect world, you'll lean toward a dribble for about for each 16 sq. in. or on the other hand extra to limit any dry zones in the media.

As the water goes down through the media, it will disseminate itself outward by means of slender activity, so exceptionally that as it ventures lower, every one of the media is absolutely soggy. Play with the clock putting to see that you get the good equilibrium of dampness while keeping off irregular dry season conditions. Water will be caught in a supply underneath and afterward reused over the media.

If utilizing trickle, utilize an in-line screen to eliminate particles from the water and hinder stopping of the producers or progressing in years the siphon. The actual pellets will do a lot of disposal of particulates. Green growth are normally occurring in water particularly where nutrients are involved. An in-line show or channel can assist with taking out green growth, notwithstanding, you'll have to smooth

it periodically.

Leaving nutrients in the water repository make green growth and the green growth limit the viability of your supplements. Keep light out of the water tank holding supplements and clean it often.

THE NUTRIENT SYSTEM

Getting the right supplements to the foundations of your plants' foundations is what's truly going on with aqua-farming. The science behind plant sustenance is very muddled and right away, can appear to be exceptionally overwhelming yet it isn't important to turn into a plant researcher to will grasps with what you should know to be a fruitful cultivator. It will, nonetheless, help to know a portion of the rudiments so you have a thought of what is happening and what that large number of synthetic substances are.

There are various supplements that a plant expects to develop and without which they will before long bite the dust. The three fundamental supplements are called macronutrients while a variety of different supplements are required yet in a lot more modest quantities.

The three macronutrients are:

Nitrogen (N): utilized in the creation of chlorophyll and amino acids. Phosphate(P): utilized in the creation of sugars, energy, blossoms, and organic product. Potassium (K): utilized in the creation of sugars starch, roots, and general hardiness.

These three parts are generally recorded most conspicuously on containers or parcels of supplements and given in numbers corresponding to their amount so if you somehow happened to see 15:9:12 you would realize their extents were fifteen percent Nitrogen, nine percent Phosphate and twelve percent Potassium. That would make up 36% of the blend in with the rest of given over to water and micronutrients. It ought to be noticed that the three figures are generally provided in a similar request NPK albeit the level of each will shift as per its planned usage.

In tank-farming, the supplements most ordinarily provided arrive in a powdered or a concentrated fluid structure which you would then weaken as per guidelines of the maker. As I would like to think, and that of numerous different cultivators, the fluid structure is by a wide margin the most functional and simple to use.
As I have proactively referenced the supply ought to be a tank that doesn't allow in light to decrease the chance of form and green growth develop. This supply ought to be essentially the very size as the pots or plate that it is taking care of and conceivably greater. Try not to blend the supplements in the repository yet add them after

premixing with water.

The Importance Of The pH Level

The pH level of your water is vital as it can negatively affect the supplement take up in the event that it is either excessively high or excessively low. Preferably, you need it to be somewhere in the range of 5.5 and 7.0. A lot of chlorine can likewise have antagonistic impacts so that also should be managed. In the event that you stand water in a pail for 24 hours the chlorine will breakdown. Then again, you can purchase refined water which appears to be somewhat of a misuse of cash to me or you can get water which will be without chlorine and is by all accounts the most consistent answer for the chlorine issue. Try not to be excessively occupied by chlorine levels as they don't kill plants and water that has represented 24 hours will in general be fine.

The pH is generally normally impacted by how much calcium it contains. An excessive amount of calcium prompts hard water and a high pH. This will need to be tested with a pH tester and if it falls outside of the given range then you can add some drops of a chemical for raising it or another for lowering it depending on the reading you are getting. All aqua-farming providers sell a two-section unit for raising and bringing down pH. Essentially weaken a couple of drops of either to one or the other raise or lower the pH to the expected level. Do this blending in a little at a time and then let the water settle prior to testing once more. It is great to have an overall thought of the pH of your water when you initially start yet after that the greater part of the pH, testing ought to be done after you have added the different supplements as these will additionally change the pH levels. The advanced testing gadget, a piece like a thermometer, is very modest and easy to use.

One method for making your life more straightforward is to have a subsequent repository. One will be being used and the other will be full with simply water. This will guarantee that the water is at a similar temperature so the plants don't need to manage an unexpected temperature change and will likewise mean you are liberated from any chlorine assuming utilizing mains regular water. Attempt to constantly utilize lukewarm water at around 18°C yet don't make this a significant issue as you will have to the point of having the opportunity to grasps with at the moment.

Once you have your water pretty much pH impartial the time has come to begin blending your supplements and for the second I am simply going to manage reason purchased aqua-farming supplements. They ordinarily come in three sections which are

blended by the maker's directions for the plants that you are developing. They will generally accompany an outline for a scope of plants and with seven days by week dose as indicated by the age of the plants. Before all else, you will need to follow this outline intently yet as your experience levels increment you will almost certainly begin trying different things with plans of your own. Practically all aquaculture grounds-keepers foster their plans and begin to add a progression of extra items that they all swear is awesome for the plants they desire to create. I will get into a portion of those added substances late yet for the present, we will simply adhere to the blending of the essential three-section nutrients.

Once you have the three containers and have observed the suitable piece of the outline that applies to your plants and the phase of development they are at you should blend them. Don't simply toss them all into a container and stir them generally up. In solid focus, they can respond with each other and make an impact called hindering that restrains their adequacy. All things considered, place a couple of liters of water in a container that is a similar size as your supply. This water should be without chlorine and to the right pH. Of course, if you have the second reservoir already prepared then that will be perfect. Pour the right measure of the initial supplement into an estimating container and afterward empty it into the water. Presently wash out the container and stand by two minutes prior to rehashing the method with the subsequent supplement. At long last, rehash the cycle with the third supplement. Recollect you should clean out the estimating recepticle between supplements to abstain from hindering. It is additionally conceivable to buy some modest estimating needles and utilize a different one for every supplement to keep away from any chance of blending them up.

Once I have every one of my supplements in the repository and I have held up a little while subsequent to adding the three then I provide the repository with somewhat of a mix. At this stage, I can retest my pH to guarantee the levels are still inside the acknowledged reach of
5.5 to 7.0. After some time the pH will probably crawl up somewhat as the supplements are drawn up by the plant. Since this is the case hopefully you will keep the pH only somewhat underneath unbiased so on the off chance that you can keep it to around 6.0 that sounds ideal. I then likewise test my blend utilizing another meter called a PPM meter or an EC meter and sporadically a TDC meter. Actually they all do exactly the same thing. They measure the salts in the supplement blend. PPM represents parts per million, EC represents Electrical conductivity and TDS represents absolute wanted salts. This simple to utilize little device will be utilized frequently during the developing stage as you should be continually observing your supplement blend to guarantee the plant is getting all that it requires. Having the chance to grasps with nutrient

mixes is one of the trickiest parts of hydroponic gardening and I don't want to make it appear too complicated because you can generally learn all you need to by just following the chart that comes with the mixture. Recall that every maker will have an alternate formula thus every framework will shift slightly.

What you are attempting to do with the plant changes at various seasons of its development cycle and to that end the combination of fixings continues to adjust. To begin you need a lot of nitrogen to carry the plants to a blooming stage at the earliest opportunity. Later you will lessen the nitrogen however increment the phosphates to expand the blossoming establishing and fruiting and through the interaction, your plant will require limited quantities of micronutrients. In the good 'ol days, there will typically be a powerful urge to add more supplements with the expectation that this will produce more and quicker development. A lot of supplement can be more terrible for the plant than excessively minimal supplement so in the event that you should alter the makers' suggestions attempt to continuously decide in favor less as opposed to more.

Now you have your repository to the pH you need and the supplements to the level suggested by the producer you are set to begin siphoning. Most systems require circulation at least twice a day and if you can get that up to once every two hours without waterlogging the plants that would be even better. You ought to utilize your meter to actually look at the supplements each a few days. If they start to get low then you can add a top-up mix which is essentially a mild version of the mixes you are using without the micronutrients. The reason for this is that the plants use a lot of the macronutrients and only very little of the micronutrients. Assuming you add more micronutrient it develops in the framework and becomes poisonous to the plants. Open air units should not be presented to rain that will weaken the water in the system.

Timing And Management

Every fourteen days you ought to supplant the supplement blend out and out. It is protected to pour the old blend onto any dirt nursery plants you have. Prior to making up the following blend clear out the repository in with heated water or weakened fade. You are then prepared to begin another bunch gave the water is sans chlorine. This is additionally a fun chance to really look at the remainder of the framework to make sure that everything is working and there is no indication of green growth. Give specific consideration to fog heads assuming you are involving them as they are effectively obstructed by micronutrient fabricate up.

Although I have proposed checking your unit you ought to really look at your plants consistently to guarantee that they are solid and sound and not giving any indications of stress. They will likewise tell you rapidly assuming that there is any issue with the framework. At the point when you have reaped your yield then it is smart to strip the whole unit down and give everything an exhaustive cleansing.

To Recap:

By now you might be beginning to feel like you have been barraged with excessively much data particularly in the event that aqua-farming is something you have never managed. The entire thought is to guarantee that you get a supplement rich fluid to the foundations of your plants with an almost impartial pH. On the off chance that you center around those needs you won't go excessively far off-base. To do this you will require an EC meter for the salts or supplements and a pH meter. You can purchase genuinely modest units that do the two estimations for you so it is easy to actually take a look at the levels. You ought to actually take a look at your blend one time each day. Limited scope units will generally vary more than bigger ones so the home cultivator must be similarly as aware of changes as the enormous scope producer.

In case of pH getting too high or too low then add a couple of drops of the suitable item in the wake of weakening. There are two items you can purchase for this and they plainly express that they are either for raising or bringing down the pH. You shouldn't attempt to change the pH more than 0.5 in one or the other course in one day as you might stun the plants. As you began with the right pH balance bigger changes are improbable.

The EC meter will provide you with a perusing of the conductivity of the water-in light of how much salts that it contains. Focus on a degree of somewhere in the range of 1.2 and 2.0. If it goes above this you can dilute the mix by adding water and if it goes below then you can top it up with top-up according to the manufacturer's instructions. I trust that works on this section for you.

WHAT TO GROW IN YOUR GARDEN

One of the incredible benefits of tank-farming is the wide assortment of yields that you can develop. In numerous ways the decision is perpetual yet you really do have to think about the requirements forced on you by the size of your unit and the space that it is in. If you are a large producer in a greenhouse set up you will probably want to concentrate on a small range of crops that sell easily and if you are a home grower working in an apartment then perhaps it is best to focus on just the crops that you buy most of. For the little maker, a decent spot to begin is dependably with lettuce as it is a serving of mixed greens crop that is eaten by a lot of westerners everyday. Additionally a harvest occupies little room and tastes better newly picked.

What Can You Grow Hydroponically?

People ask much of the time, "what would I be able to develop hydroponically? The answer is in all actuality very straightforward: You can grow an enormous scope of blossoms, vegetables, and spices hydroponically, aside from mushrooms that are fungi.

Following is an agenda of numerous vegetation that grows pleasantly in aqua-farming frameworks, along for certain measurements of interest:

Flowers

Growing blossoms loans itself incredibly to aquaculture cultivating as they can be filled en masse, and can be developed all year. Most blossoms will do appropriately in a tank-farming nursery, and when seedlings are adequately large, vegetation can be diminished or transplanted.

Herbs

Many spices will foster very well in an aqua-farming setting. Some that do the good include anise, basil, catnip, chamomile, chervil, chives, cilantro, coriander, dill, fennel, lavender, marjoram, mint, oregano, parsley, rosemary, sage, tarragon, and thyme.

Anise

Anise is a padded yearly that develops from 1 to 2 ft high, has finely cut

serrated leaves and tiny, whitish vegetation in level bunches. Both the leaves and seeds have a warm, sweets licorice taste. It develops quickly from seed and should be planted after all danger of ice has passed. The unpracticed leaves can be decreased each time vegetation is goliath enough and seeds might be assembled multi month after vegetation sprout. Anise leaves can be utilized in servings of mixed greens and as a trimming; the seeds flavor sweets like treats and cookies.

Basil

In a covered climate, creating basil can be done during the year. Once adult, it very well may be gathered and managed week after week. It answers very appropriately to tank-farming growing.

Cannabis

A psyche changing spice got from the blooming first rate of hemp plants. Pot is controlled under Schedule I of the Controlled Substances Act of 1970. It is moreover known as bhang, weed, grass, ganja, cannabis, pot, dope, tea, and weed. It flourishes and develops to an additional a lively plant in an aqua-farming framework. Most pot plants developed in the United States begin to blossom via late

August to early October and the blossoms are reaped from October to November.

Rosemary

A strong evergreen sub-bush developed fundamentally for fragrant leaves are utilized in culinary flavoring and yield an oil once utilized in medication. Little gentle blue vegetation are borne in April or May. The foliage is white and wooly on the under aspect and dull and striking above. Plants can create to a top of 6 toes and extreme for a really long time yet need security from the virus. It favors alkalic soil and full sun yet endures moderate shade. Plant in seed lofts 22 weeks before deal in 10 cm distance across pots. Seeds to completed plugs, 12 weeks; fittings to saleable plants, 10 weeks.

Sage

A typical title for the tough sub-bush that is impressively developed for preparing dressings utilized with well off meats, and for seasoning wieners and cheddar. In aquaculture, it very well may be developed from seeds covered from cold and it inclines toward full sun. As the vegetation regularly surpass 3 ft in breadth, they must be developed essentially that some distance separated. Sage leaves ought to be harvested

prior to blossoming and dried in a very much ventilated room on screens or in a business dryer, away from direct daylight and afterward shop in impenetrable holders. Plant in attachments or seed pads 12 to 14 weeks sooner than the deal. Seeds to finished plugs, two months; attachments to saleable plants, four to 6 weeks.

Tarragon

A lasting spice the leaves of which are utilized for preparing, specifically, vinegar. Tarragon develops to a few ft tall and preferences moderate sun, leaning toward some tone all through the most exceptional part of the day. Tarragon, at some stage in development, seems to have little fragrance; yet after the leaves or tops are collected, the oils tune in and start transmitting their unique tarragon candy smell. Fittings to saleable plants, 7 weeks.

Thyme

A plant of the mint family lengthy developed and esteemed as a treats spice. It has little lavender or purple vegetation and is developed as a boundary plant, for decoration, or as a spice to utilized for season. Thyme ought to be planted in late-winter. It is solid and can develop under most circumstances. It favors full sun. Thyme needs minimal preparation once full-filled in a very agribusiness framework. Sow in plugs 12 to 14 weeks sooner than deal. Seeds to finished plugs, 6 to about two months; fittings to saleable plants, four to 6 weeks.

Watercress

Low creating and following European lasting, an individual from the mustard family. It is without issues developed from seed. Its natural season is from mid-pre-winter until spring. After its blossom buds seem the passes on become too rank in taste to be palatable. It is furthermore easily filled inside in an aquaculture framework. Begin verdure with seed by utilizing planting delicately in pots loaded down with a medium. Watercress has numerous culinary, embellishing, and restorative uses.

Vegetables

Vegetables that had best in a very horticulture garden incorporate artichokes, beans, lettuce, spinach, cabbage, beets, asparagus, broccoli, cauliflower, Brussels fledglings, and peas. Vegetables that develop at a lower place the dirt, similar to onions, leeks, carrots, parsnips, potatoes, sweet potatoes, and radishes will develop hydroponically, notwithstanding, they will boot need bigger consideration. A vegetation to avoid are corn, zucchini, mid year squash, and vining plants. They can be filled in an aqua-farming nursery, yet they are currently not housed

proficiently, and basically as of now not useful. They will rule your entire unit. Your sources are higher spent on crops more noteworthy ideal to the minimized systems.

MAINTENANCE OF THE HYDROPONIC GARDEN

Eventually, even the most fundamental aquaculture nurseries will require some upkeep. Hydroponic system maintenance includes everything from monitoring and adjusting nutrient concentrations to regularly flushing the system, and even the occasional scrubbing of pots and reservoirs.

Managing The Nutrient Solution

There are multiple ways of dealing with an aqua-farming supplement arrangement. Picking the administration procedure for your aqua-farming nursery will rely upon crop choice, supply size, garden plan, and individual inclination. I frequently pick the choice that requires minimal measure of time regardless of whether that could somewhat influence development rate or yield quality, yet you might wish to deal with your supplements all the more near improve development. The accompanying administration procedures are coordinated by the work they require.

Least Effort: Set and Forget
Build the repository with the suggested compost rate per gallon recorded on the manure pack/bottle. Change the pH in the event that it is far outside of the objective reach, or don't. Permit the yield to develop until it is prepared to gather or until the water level is excessively low for plants to get to the supplement arrangement. This technique can turn out extraordinary for mixed greens in drifting pontoon frameworks and may work in different frameworks assuming they have an adequately enormous supply comparative with the quantity of plants developing. I've grown an astounding number of awesome looking yields utilizing this negligible exertion methodology. This administration style can have issues when utilized with crops that have long development cycles, like tomatoes, peppers, cucumbers, and other blooming crops. Assuming you wish to utilize negligible exertion and develop crops that make some more extended memories until development, attempt this method.

Little Effort: Top Off
This strategy is like set and neglect, however as the water level drops the cultivator basically adds water to keep up with the first level. Over the long run this strategy will weaken the supplement focus in the repository and supplement inadequacies might show up on the yield. This technique can work for quick growing

crops with low supplement requests like microgreens, mixed greens, and a few spices. This method sometimes works for some larger crops depending on the system, but there is some risk of overdiluting the nutrient solution, especially when using a small reservoir.

Some Effort: Top Off And Amend
The most widely recognized strategy for keeping a supplement arrangement

in a tank-farming nursery is to finish off the repository as referenced in the past strategy, then add more manure to the supply to keep an objective EC. Please see the appendix for example target ECs for common hydroponic crops. In the wake of adding manure to arrive at the objective EC, the producer changes the pH of the supplement arrangement utilizing either a corrosive (pH down) or base (pH up). There are some simple to-utilize pH down and pH up items accessible in develop stores, and there are DIY choices that are regularly less ideal however usable. For pH down, a few aqua-farming landscapers use vinegar or lemon juice and for pH up, some utilization baking soda.

To finish off and revise the arrangement in your framework, you will require an EC meter, tank-farming manure, an estimating cup, a pH meter, pH down and pH up corrections, and a pipette (eyedropper).

Flushing

EC is an extraordinary general reference for supplement content in an aqua-farming repository, yet tragically, it doesn't recount the entire story. Not all supplements are taken up by plants at a similar rate. After some time, a few supplements will gather and others will be quickly exhausted, bringing about an imbalanced supplement arrangement. Large commercial hydroponic farms send out water samples to testing facilities to get exact quantities of each nutrient in the reservoir and the grower then adjusts the manure inputs accordingly. To play out these compost changes requires complex science and a profound comprehension of a harvest's particular supplement prerequisites. The far-simpler option is to occasionally flush an aquaculture framework. Flushing is the most common way of eliminating the current supplement arrangement and topping off the framework with freshwater and afterward adding new manure. The recurrence of flushing is subject to many elements, including crop, climate, framework, fertilizer, and water quality. Most landscapers make progress utilizing the accompanying guideline to sort out flush recurrence: "Flush a repository when the amount of water added to finish off a supply is comparable to the size of the reservoir."

Example: A 40-gallon supply loses 5 gallons every day to evapotranspiration

(plant happening and supply dissipation). The producer adds 5 gallons to the repository day to day to finish off the supply for water misfortune. Following 8 days the producer adds an aggregate of 40 gallons (8 days × 5 gallons = 40 gallons), a similar volume of water as the first repository size. The cultivator ought to flush the supply each 8 days.

This guideline is extremely moderate and numerous producers can flush less often while utilizing conventional tank-farming manures. This standard is helpful, nonetheless, for getting an overall rule. The water flushed from a tank-farming framework shouldn't be put down the channel. Numerous grounds-keepers utilize the old supplement answer for water their pruned plants, raised beds, yard, or trees. A customary nursery is an incredible ally to an aqua-farming nursery, and it tends to be a permanent spot for old supplement arrangements, treated the soil plants, and substrates.

Cleaning

Hydroponic cultivators can utilize an assortment of items to disinfect their nurseries. The most secure and least demanding choice is generally dish cleanser. A few extra choices accessible to side interest aquaculture cultivators incorporate family fade (utilize 1/2 to 1 ounce for each gallon of water), isopropyl liquor (70% or more grounded), and hydrogen peroxide (3% is by and large adequate; more grounded fixations are accessible yet they should be maneuvered carefully, so read and follow item labels).

It is ideal to clean a tank-farming nursery while it is as yet wet. Stains, plant roots, and leaves are more hard to eliminate when dry. If conceivable, detach any siphons or air stones to clean freely from the reservoir.

Beneficial Insects

Some sorts of honey bees are helpful as pollinators, despite the fact that they for the most part just successfully fertilize plants from a similar area of beginning, making it more straightforward for some plants to duplicate and deliver organic product. Additionally, a few honey bees are savage or parasitic and kill bug pests.

This gathering incorporates honey bees as well as numerous different species that are more effective at fertilization. Bees can be attracted to many companion plants, especially bee balm and pineapple sage for honeybees or Apiaceae such as Queen Ana's lace and parsley for predatory bees.

Ladybugs are by and large thought to be helpful in light of the fact that they eat a lot of aphids, bugs, and different arthropods that feed on various plants.

Ladybug

The most normally delivered and unmistakable valuable bug for amateurs and progressed is the ladybug (Hippodamia convergens). Ladybugs are generalists and eat aphids, whiteflies, vermin, weevils, blue-bloods, and other scarab hatchlings. They like and will search for aphids to exploit them. A grown-up ladybug eats up to 60 aphids per day and up to 5,000 during its life. Ladybugs frequently come in plastic compartments with 1,500 bugs. Bigger bundles are accessible with up to 50,000 insects.

To take advantage of your ladybug discharge, water plants and leaves first. Ladybugs as a rule come in their compartments with food yet not water and are probably going to search for a beverage when it is delivered. A drop of water close to your ideal objective will assist you with remaining there to take care of your business. Ladybugs for the most part don't fly into the evening, so it is alluring to deliver your bundle at sunset or later.

It is generally awesome and exceptionally powerful to deliver a moderate sum in your developing regions. An invasion or episode of a specific kind of irritation might require the arrival of a large number of ladybugs. In any case, in any case, something like a couple for every square foot of grounds might be delivered, or an overpopulation might compel them to search for another food, or more terrible, starve to death.

Delphastus Catalinae

They are comparative with the normal ladybird, yet it is a lot more modest. These small

round brown-dark scarabs are the size of a pencil tip. Not at all like ladybugs, they can't keep a populace without prey. Ladies need to consume somewhere in the range of 100 and 150 whitefly eggs day to day to acquire and hold their egg-laying capacities. Both male and female Delphastus eat whiteflies at all stages, including at the grown-ups and fairies stages. They kill all of their prey by gnawing and making openings in the body of the grown-up or youthful whitefly and separating their substance, leaving an empty, shell-molded body.

Each D-Catalinae can eat up to 10,000 whiteflies in the course of its life. They can be utilized with a helpful parasite since they don't consume parasitic whiteflies. The best outcomes with these scarabs are accomplished assuming more than ten are delivered at every whitefly hot spot.

Praying Mantis

Another hunter that is frequently utilized for bug species is the asking mantis (Genus Stagmomantis, which happens in America). Supplicating mantises are sold in their egg containers. Those cases ought to be hanged close to bother issues plants. The arising mantis will be prepared to eat an assortment of little irritation species. At the point when they mature, they will eat moths, houseflies and mosquitoes. While incubating, imploring mantises ought to be isolated in light of the fact that they can be savages at a youthful age.

Contrary to mainstream thinking, government regulation forbidding killing or moving mantis doesn't exist. They are not a jeopardized species. Assuming you are sufficiently fortunate to observe a supplicating mantis egg enclose the wild, get it and spot it in your developing area.

Green Lacewings

Like the asking mantis that is outside in your nursery, green wings (Chrysoperla rufilabris) are a typical open air hunter that can be joined into your indoor bug control schedule. They eat an assortment of bugs however are keen on aphids and dinner bugs. Without their #1 prey, they eat whiteflies and textured insects.

Adults lay their eggs some place close to a potential wellspring of food. It is the hatchlings of the tip wing that have the main impact on bother control. Chrysoperla is generally usually offered as an egg or hatchling because of its youthful

craving. Hatchlings should be delivered on receipt as they become savages without prey. Assuming they are acquired as eggs, keep them off the ground or where they can be inclined to hunters. The subterranean insects eat the eggs. Green Crisopas are known to nibble individuals, yet this is intriguing, and their chomps are non-toxic.

Insidious flower insects

'Orius insidiosus' or slippery blossom bugs are named after their outrageous forcefulness towards thrips. They stand before different kinds of bugs and are an especially valuable nuisance control choice, as they are covered in shut bloom buds looking for food on the off chance that they can't be found in the leaves or on the other hand assuming they have proactively devoured light harvests.

InsidiOus blossom bugs are just helpful in the mid year months since they require regular light and warmth. Counterfeit lighting, also as extra warmth, can be utilized to grow the value when required. For the most part, they are sold in 500 units and are applied all the more successfully straightforwardly to pervaded plants. Like the green tip, O. insidiosus can chomp individuals, however it seldom happens.

Hypoaspis miles

'Hypoaspis miles' are a sort of soil parasite that can be set straightforwardly in the center of plants free from holders or straightforwardly in the

encompassing soil. They can be utilized in breaks in substantial floors or joints of block or stone floors and are a decent choice for controlling bugs for mushroom creation. Their essential food is thrips and pupa hatchlings, however they likewise assist with battling parasite mosquitoes by eating their eggs and hatchlings. Water the locale before it is delivered and afterward again a couple of hours after the fact. They're generally accessible in 25,000 piece quantities.

Atheta coriaria

'Atheta coriaria', also called ground bug, is one more hunter that lives on the ground like the Hypoaspis. These little, frequently regular creepy crawlies flourish in damp and dull regions, where they can benefit from mosquito hatchlings and pupae, bank flies, and thrips. Flying bugs will fly looking for new food whenever they have depleted their unique area, so they are valuable for complete inclusion. These are generally sold in 100 units and can be incorporated into the media of manure, rock, or soil.

Nematodes

Nematodes are tiny worms whose standing is regularly awful. There are many sorts of hurtful nematodes however valuable sorts as well. The stone nematode is a types of nematode that, when fused into the dirt, have some control over mosquitoes, thrips, and in excess of 200 types of flying and slithering bugs. They do this by taking advantage of their bug casualties at the larval stage.

When they are as yet filling in the dirt to benefit from them, they look for those bugs. A grown-up nematode can possibly deliver up to 200,000 posterity north of a while. At the point when they are prepared to replicate, they discharge their prey and lay their eggs in it. Whenever they are conceived, youthful nematodes feed on the host species from within and afterward arise to track down their prey.

Nematode bundles are sold with a huge number of dynamic units (AU) each. They can be inserted in granules or chips made of vermiculite, which can be effectively fused into the dirt media. They can likewise be bundled and delivered in a soggy wipe blended in with water system water or in a powder that can be utilized as an earth shower. Nematodes can be put away refrigerated for quite a long time before use.

Aphidoletes Aphidimyza

Carnivorous outsiders that show up in the sci-fi films from the tummies of their human hosts depend on realities - this happens in the bug world between have aphids and their parasitic executioner Aphidoletes aphidimyza. The aphids are normally gotten as pupae and set in an open compartment close to plants with high aphid content.

Once the aphids are pupated, they will search out and penetrate in aphids to take care of. Anybody can kill up to 65 aphids per day and kill a greater number of aphids than they can consume. The aphids leave supposed aphid mummies, which are connected to the leaf of the plant where they tracked down it. These mummies are the emptied out cadavers of aphids and furthermore fill in as a cover in which the grown-up aphids lay their eggs.

Encarsia Formosa

Encarsia Formosa is a sort of little, parasitic wasp that loves just to lay its eggs in the hatchlings of the whitefly. The whitefly hatchling is situated on the underside of the leaves. When the Encarsia Formosa eggs have been

infused, the impacted hatchlings seem like little dull scales from which the grown-up wasp arises. Encarsia is generally sold as dolls that are stuck on a punch card that is set in a plant that is swarmed with grown-up whiteflies. Encarsia cards or different transporters ought to be involved week after week for as long as 10 weeks, regardless of whether no whiteflies are visible.

Bait

A different except for compelling natural technique for bother control, particularly for thrips, is the utilization of draws that are teased with a pheromone of sexual animosity created by male thrips. These are normally utilized alongside a little, tacky snare coin. Thrips are drawn to the blue tone. A little container containing the pheromone is put on the lower part of the card, and afterward the card is hung almost a swarmed plant.

The pheromone sets off the mating response in both male and female thrips and squares them from benefiting from your plants. These cards and snares ought to be utilized against weighty invasion. They ought to be business as usual irritation control. Helpful bugs ought to be utilized related to the traps to control serious thrip outbreaks.

Predatory mite (Mesoseiulus longipes)

The most exceedingly awful vermin bug an indoor cultivator can contract is the feared bug parasite. Ruthless bugs just search for and feed on bug vermin. The indoor landscaper has a few unique sorts of ruthless vermin accessible. *Mesoseiulus longipes are the most ideal for most indoor nursery conditions.*

They have the most broad scope of favored stickiness and temperature, however in particular, they observe lower mugginess levels (most indoor nurseries) adequate for reproduction.

Other Beneficial Insect Tips

Bed bugs feed on spoiling natural material and don't represent a danger in the nursery except if there is overpopulation. For this situation, marvels can regularly tackle the problem.

The mulch can go about as a hindrance to awful bugs or as a magnet for good bugs. For instance, weighty straw cushioning keeps many sorts of bugs out, the greater part of which are destructive, and cushioning with roughage or dry grass is an extraordinary method for drawing in spiders.

Familiarizing yourself with the bugs that visit your nursery is the best safeguard against hurtful bugs. Pesticides can hurt both valuable bugs and plants and can be risky whenever utilized inappropriately. Assuming you consolidate an assortment of important plants and great invite bugs to your nursery, you can allow them to do all the work.

Precautions

Predators and valuable irritations are utilized all the more successfully as a component of a standard support program. Trusting that nuisances will happen or swarm in the indoor developing region is past the time to be successful. Gainful bugs don't fill in as fast as substance insect sprays, however they can be as successful, while perhaps not more whenever given sufficient opportunity to land their position done.

Both valuable bugs are powerless against a considerable lot of similar insect poisons (natural or not) used to oversee them like the nuisance types. By and large, they are more helpless to the utilization of pesticides as their bug partners have not laid out similar resilience to synthetic pesticides. Try not to deliver advantageous bugs previously, during, or subsequent to utilizing insecticides.

COMMON PROBLEMS AND TROUBLESHOOTING

Now that you have figured out how to be a framework manufacturer, an indoor grounds-keeper, and a support specialist, the time has come to figure out how to be a specialist. Here is a concise introduction on the best way to analyze and investigate your aqua-farming developing system.

Nutrient Deficiencies

Traditional supplement lack and poisonousness distinguishing proof aides show a solitary leaf with side effects, however these can undoubtedly lead a nursery worker to overcorrect an issue or right an issue erroneously. Regularly a supplement harmfulness or inadequacy is because of supplement arrangement/substrate pH, natural circumstances, crop age, or the presence of a microorganism. Prior to expecting the issue is supplement related, verify if:

• All plants of a similar theatrical presentation comparable symptoms.

• The pH is in the objective reach for the harvest and not low (underneath 5.0) or high (above 6.5).

• The EC is in the objective reach for the crop.

• The air temperature is inside the objective reach for the crop.

- The water temperature is inside an optimal reach for the yield, not beneath 55°F or above 85°F.
- The whole harvest is getting respectable wind current. The leaves ought to be apparently moving.
- The yield is irritation free.
- The light levels are inside the objective range.
- The supplement arrangement is made utilizing a manure intended for aqua-farming gardens.

If the response is yes to this large number of conditions, it is possible the issue is supplement related. Regularly, supplement related issues can be cured by unloading out the supplement arrangement and restarting the system.

Chlorosis And Necrosis

Chlorosis is the deficiency of chlorophyll, the green color in plants. Chlorosis can be utilized to portray leaf yellowing from many causes, including supplement inadequacies or vermin harm. Rot is plant tissue passing. Plant infections or supplement lacks frequently start with indications of chlorosis that lead to necrosis.

Interveinal Chlorosis on New Growth

Interveinal chlorosis on new development regularly demonstrates a lack of iron or another micronutrient insufficiency. Most aquaculture manures give a lot of iron, so the issue is seldom the presence of iron. Lacks of iron by and large happen on the grounds that the pH is excessively high. A few harvests are "iron-wasteful" and battle to take-up iron. Basil is one of the normal instances of an iron-wasteful plant. Assuming basil is filled in a supplement arrangement with a high pH, at times a little more than 6, it can show interveinal chlorosis on new development demonstrative of a lack of iron. The leaves showing this kind of interveinal chlorosis won't recuperate however future development can get back to business as usual on the off chance that the pH is changed and additionally iron is enhanced to the supplement solution.

Chlorosis on Older Leaves

Chlorosis on more seasoned leaves can be the consequence of perhaps one or two scenarios:

Nitrogen inadequacy Nitrogen is a significant part of chlorophyll, the green shade in leaves. Plants can take the nitrogen from chlorophyll and move it all through the plant depending on the situation. At the point when the plant distinguishes a lack of nitrogen, it will migrate the nitrogen in its more seasoned passes on to its new development. Nitrogen lacks can seem when yields are developed at a low EC. New aquaponic nurseries will now and again disapprove of nitrogen deficiencies.

Natural Senescence is the regular passing of leaves because of advanced age. In mature plants, it is entirely expected to see some lower leaves bite the dust from regular senescence. In the event that the aquaculture garden has both youthful and old plants, verify whether just the more seasoned plants are showing chlorosis on more established leaves; this would demonstrate regular senescence.

Lack of magnesium This appears to be like a lack of nitrogen with more established leaves showing chlorosis, however a lack of magnesium will have interveinal chlorosis with necrotic spots and additionally necrotic leaf edges. Most lacks of magnesium can be helped with magnesium sulfate (Epsom salt) at a pace of 1/2 to 1 teaspoon for every gallon.

Tip Burn

Tip burn is technically a calcium deficiency, but very often it appears even when there is calcium present in the nutrient solution. Calcium is basic for the development of plant cell dividers. The plant's calcium take-up can in some cases battle to stay aware of the arrangement of new cells when a plant is filling quick in a climate with extreme light and warm circumstances. There are two principle ways of helping this issue.

- Try an alternate assortment. A few assortments are extremely delicate to tip consume while others might fill fine in the current conditions.
- Try adding a few full scale components, for example, calcium and magnesium to the nutritive arrangement, that further develop plants' water flow and increment Tip Burn tolerance.

In-Depth Analysis

Tip Burn: Which information tends to the infection incited by deficient vehicle of calcium through the field however doesn't allude to indications of minimal leaf consuming on more seasoned leaves, additionally corresponded for low potassium, or the minuscule round necrotic (dead tissue) regions found on leaf drop focuses set off by gutting.

Guttation is irrelevant to calcium, starting from roots that remove cell sap from plant hydrothodes, normally if the stomata are shut for colder, all the more warm circumstances where the cF supplement turns out to be too small.

Tip consuming is the result of lacking calcium contacting the outside region of the plants and is near bloom end decay on tomatoes and consuming seen on the sides of peppers. Tip consuming will regularly happen on different ornamentals and petals from similar sources. On the off chance that plants are put under pressure, regularly during raised temperatures and dampness stress, youthful delicate development edges breakdown. Whenever the tissues full grown, the dead edges dry out and don't expand, tip consume brings about a measuring of contaminated regions. (Run of the mill injury-right
- on lettuce showing corruption and raddichio showing measuring) While low calcium levels can be related with supplement arrangements, which isn't the typical reason for tank-farming harvests. For specific conditions, inferable from lacking calcium move to establish limits in two testing circumstances. For high temperatures, sped up happening doesn't help calcium particle development. In exceptionally sticky cold conditions, insufficient transpiration
ends up conveying sufficient calcium particles into the field. Calcium is a wide compound with inconvenience passing into the plant.

Where such ominous conditions happen and speedy plant development occurs, low calcium rates can likewise result from weakening because of fast leaf extension. Weighty (over the top) nitrogen might cause this.

Temperature survey. Other lettuce and verdant plants are powerless to tip consume when plant-high temperatures surpass 10-20 minutes above 25C. Tip consume safe lettuce assortments can persevere between 27-28C. A few assortments (particularly oak leaf types) endure higher temperatures. Hazing and moistening over plants can bring down temperatures proficiently, giving low relative humidity.

This includes delicate waters or leaves turn clear with the dissolvable salts left when the water dissipates. With summer use, 35% shade regularly assists with bringing down temperatures.

Pest-Management Products And Equipment

Hydroponics can somely affect bug pressure yet the greater component on bother pressure is the climate. Aquaculture frameworks are regularly utilized in controlled conditions like nurseries or inside. Filling in a controlled climate gives the landscaper the possibility to totally prohibit bugs from the harvest, yet accomplishing this can be undeniably challenging. For the most part, a few nuisances get into the nursery and when they get in they can rapidly duplicate. A controlled climate garden is incredible for the two plants and irritations. Whenever a bug gets into an indoor nursery it winds up in a climate with amazing climate and no hunters... basically bother paradise. There are a few strategies for controlling irritations, yet regularly the best protection is anticipation. A large portion of the strategies for bother the executives can be utilized in a controlled climate or outdoors.

Preventive Methods

Preventive strategies incorporate irritation avoidance methods like positive tension develop rooms and HEPA admission channels depicted before in the Equipment for Growing Indoors area. Another rejection practice is wearing clean garments prior to going into an indoor develop space to try not to convey in bothers from outside. Preventive techniques likewise incorporate choosing plant assortments that are fitting for the developing climate and have sickness obstruction, and giving these plants the water and supplements they should be sound to the point of opposing diseases.

Physical If preventive practices don't keep bothers out and a nuisance is found in the nursery, actual bug the executives rehearses are an extraordinary, nontoxic strategy for controlling bugs. My number one actual irritation the executives method is utilizing a vacuum to eliminate any bugs I spot. Extra actual bug the board strategies are eliminating whole plants and utilizing tacky snares. Tacky snares are additionally utilized for checking vermin levels.

Biological irritation the board includes the utilization of hunters, parasites, and sicknesses to control bother populaces. One of the most well known organic bug the board systems for landscapers is the arrival of ladybugs. Natural irritation the board may not totally kill a bug populace, however it typically can keep the vermin populace in check.

Organic Pesticides Organic pesticides are for the most part viewed as less toxic

than ordinary/engineered pesticides, yet they actually ought to be utilized mindfully. Continuously look at the mark on pesticides, even natural ones, to see whether there is any suggested individual insurance hardware like gloves, goggles, or a respirator. Most ranches can totally oversee bothers utilizing just natural pesticides.

Conventional Pesticides Conventional, or engineered, pesticides are seldom expected by home landscapers. Even commercial farms that are not certified organic will very often solely use organic pesticides because they are very effective. The vast majority of the regular pesticides accessible to grounds-keepers are similarly basically as protected as natural pesticides when utilized properly.

Pest-Management Tools

This is in no way, shape or form a far reaching rundown of vermin the board apparatuses, only a couple of my number one strategies for overseeing irritations in my garden.

Vacuum This is a without pesticide strategy for eliminating insects.

Sticky Traps Yellow tacky snares are for the most part used to trap and screen aphids, whiteflies, and organism gnats. Blue tacky snares are for the most part used to trap and screen thrips.

Beneficial Insects Successfully overseeing vermin with normal hunters can be interesting. There are numerous valuable bug choices; coming up next are a couple of the most regularly involved hunters in-home aquaculture gardens. Develop room environment and the presence of splash buildups can affect the viability of useful insects.

- Lacewing (Chrysoperla carnea): Primarily used to control aphids yet additionally might be powerful for controlling whiteflies and thrips.
- Ladybug (Coccinella septempunctata): Used to control aphids.
- Praying mantis (Tenodera Sinensis): Eats a wide scope of bugs, including aphids.
- Predatory parasite (Neoseiulus cucumeris): Used to control thrips and bug mites.
- Swirski vermin (Amblyseius swirskii): Used to control thrips.

Essential Oils Essential oils can be extremely successful for killing or repulsing bugs like bugs, thrips, and aphids. A couple of the more usually utilized medicinal oils are garlic, clove, mint, thyme, rosemary, and cinnamon.

Neem Oil A natural pesticide got from the neem tree, this oil can repulse bugs and conceivably kill them whenever applied straightforwardly onto the pest.

Azadirachtin A concentrate produced using Neem seeds that concentrates one of

the most powerful insecticidal mixtures found in Neem oil. Azadirachtin repulses bugs like Neem oil, however it additionally upsets the shedding system in numerous vermin. Azadirachtin keeps bothers in their adolescent stage, keeping them from arriving at adulthood and reproducing.

Organic Pyrethrins A natural pesticide got from the chrysanthemum bloom. One of the most remarkable natural pesticides, it is able to do rapidly killing most bugs when applied at a solid fixation. Pyrethrins may conceivably kill useful bugs too.

Bacillus thuringiensis (Bt) A gainful microorganism basically used to oversee caterpillars.

Bacillus thuringiensis subspecies israelensis (Bti) A subspecies of Bt that can give some organic control of growth gnats.

Soap Insecticidal cleansers, or even dish cleanser, can be exceptionally successful for controlling whiteflies and aphids.

Spinosad An organic pesticide derived from the bacterium *Saccharopolyspora Spinosa*. Powerful for controlling thrips and caterpillars.

Streptomyces lydicus An advantageous microorganism that is successful against root decay and foliar fungi.

Potassium Bicarbonate An extremely viable natural fungicide prepared to do rapidly thumping down fine mold issues. May likewise be utilized to bring pH up in tank-farming systems.

Sodium Bicarbonate (baking pop) Very like potassium bicarbonate insufficiency against fine buildup. Plants can endure a few sodium, yet they will show supplement poisonousness or lack side effects when presented to over the top amounts.

Many grounds-keepers can utilize sodium bicarbonate to really control fine mold and other foliar fungi.

As soon as you have decided the reason for the sickness or which vermin is available, take quick, remedial activities to control them to forestall their spread. Utilize supported compound splashes. Look for the utilization of normal pesticides (bioagents). In the event that these are not adequately compelling, apply more grounded ones. Don't over and again apply similar pesticides in later pervasions; change the sort of pesticides to limit any conceivable opposition develop by the vermin. A far better methodology is to present regular hunters (helpful bugs) into the yield that will eat or parasitize the bugs keeping their numbers restricted. These useful bugs are accessible through various wholesalers and even

aqua-farming outlets. Yet again there is a ton of data accessible on the Internet.

When choosing assortments, you ought to pick safe assortments against infections. The utilization of safe assortments will rearrange and expand your prosperity. While aqua-farming development incredibly decreases the danger of illness in the substrate, it doesn't forestall infections in the plant development over the substrate. Keeping up with ideal natural circumstances and controlling vermin will help enormously in the avoidance of sicknesses.

When you think a sickness is available begin to recognize explicit regions on the plant that are impacted and portray the idea of the symptoms.

Firstly, distinguish the region impacted: leaves, blossoms, organic product, developing tip, stem, crown region, or roots. It could be a mix of these. For instance, in the event that the plant shrinks during the high light and temperature times of the day, likely the roots are tainted lessening water take-up. Slice a roots to decide if they are bloated and white or delicate and foul. Assuming the last option, you know promptly there is a root problem.

Is the general plant structure hindered or predominated? Is the highest point of the plant exceptionally thick with many little leaves and short internodes?

Look for the accompanying side effects: twisted, badly crumpled, rolled, twisted, mottled, chlorotic, necrotic pamphlets. Look for the presence of spots-concentric or curved, white, powdery, hair-like growth on the leaves (due to some fungi, such as powdery mildew and Botrytis).

Cut the stem on a plant to see if the vascular tissue is clear and white or brown and delicate that would demonstrate the presence of a sickness living being.
Any staining or non-abrasiveness at the collar (crown) of the plant would demonstrate an infection. A natural product might be distorted or have spots or sores highlighting the presence of an illness. In the wake of portraying and taking more time for future reference of these side effects go onto sites of the Internet to find photographs and portrayals of illness side effects that might be like those of your plants.

Leaf mold (Cladosporium)
It begins as a little dark spot on the underside of the leaf and ventures into a

pale region on the upper surface. Great disinfection, ventilation, and temperatures forestalling high dampness lessen possible disease. A few viable fungicides are available.

Early blight (Alternaria and Septoria):
Dead spots show up on leaves, going after more seasoned leaves first. Ventilation lessens disease, Remove lower leaves as plants are brought down to increment air flow hence making lower relative humidity.

Gray mold (Botrytis):

These parasitic spores enter wounds. That is the justification for cutting leaves with a sharp blade or pruning shears to get a perfect surface that will mend rapidly. Dark form shows up as a damp decay with a feathery silver (bushy like) development over the contaminated region. A few fungicides have some control over the disease at its beginning phase before the growth annihilates (supports) the whole plant stem.

Viruses:

Most nursery assortments have opposition or resistance to numerous infections. Decrease possible disease by controlling sucking bugs that are vectors (aphids, bugs, whiteflies). Since tomatoes, eggplants, and peppers are of the Solanaceous family, they are inclined to similar sicknesses. Tomatoes and eggplants are of the genera Solanum as are intently related.

This family likewise incorporates vegetables, for example, potatoes and some flowers.

Gray form (Botrytis): This is the most pervasive illness of eggplants. Keep up with ideal mugginess levels through ventilation and temperature. De-leafing lower, yellowing leaves will help with keeping the mugginess close to the plant base low. Make a total separation or cut at the foundation of the leaf petiole (where the leaf joins the stem). Botrytis will likewise influence organic products, stems, and leaves. Cut the organic product during gathering with a pruning shears or sharp blade to make a quick recuperating of the injury. Subsequent to blooming eliminate dead blossoms that poor person set natural product as regularly Botrytis rapidly attacks these dead tissues.

Stem decay (Sclerotinia): This is a parasite that contaminates the stem of eggplants. Treat it with respect to Botrytis. Practice great disinfection and ventilation. Both dim form and stem decay happen on peppers. Medicines are equivalent to for eggplants
and tomatoes. Some infections likewise may taint peppers. The best advance is anticipation by end of sucking insects.

Powdery mold: This is the most widely recognized sickness on cucumbers. Little white spots show up on the upper leaf surface. It spreads quickly to local leaves and plants. Spots expand and spread to cover the whole leaf surface as the illness advances. Appropriate sterilization and ventilation help with forestalling this sickness. Basic sulfur disintegrated by a warmer will make a cloud that can enter all regions inside the harvest. This is by and large done expedite. The best solution for this sickness is the determination of safe or exceptionally open minded assortments like Dominica, Logica, and Marillo. Fine buildup is particularly irresistible under tropical, damp conditions.

Gummy stem curse (Didymella bryoniae): This sickness of blossoms, creating organic product, petiole, and base of the principle stem is communicated as tan-hued sores. Great ventilation and ideal relative mugginess will put contamination by this parasite down. A few fungicides will capture the infection.

Cucumber mosaic infection (CMV): Some strains of this infection likewise contaminate tomatoes. Impacted leaves become overshadowed, long, and slender. There is no fix, just counteraction through sterilization and annihilation of sucking bugs. There are numerous cucumber cultivars now impervious to this infection. They are shown by the code CMV after the assortment name.

Bacterial delicate decay (Erwinia carotovora): This is a bacterium. It causes decaying of the inside piece of the head as it structures and furthermore at the crown of the plant. Ideal ventilation to keep up with ideal dampness levels helps in decreasing this infection. Sterilization among crops and during creation assists with limiting any infection.

Lettuce enormous vein (Mirafiori lettuce infection): Symptoms are developed, clear veins of the leaves. Leaves become unsettled and twisted apparently. Sterilization and safe assortments are the method for prevention.

Pests

Whiteflies: This is the most irksome nuisance related with tomatoes. You can without much of a stretch recognize this bug by its white wings and body. It is most pervasive on the undersides of leaves and flies rapidly when upset. There are helpful bugs as well as pesticides accessible for their control.

Aphids: These nuisances are quite often found in your terrace garden. They are green, brown, or dark relying on the species. Their distinctive pear-formed body places them separated from different bugs. There are winged and wingless structures. One unmistakable attribute of their pervasion on plants is the presence of "honeydew" discharged from their midsections causing tenacity of leaves and plant parts as they suck on the plants. This fluid draws in insects, so assuming you experience enormous subterranean insect populaces around the plants it very well may be because of the presence of aphids.

Often dirty molds (growths) taint the leaves as an auxiliary creature, making a dark film on the leaves.

Two-spotted bug vermin: Mites are connected with bugs and ticks. They have four sets of legs contrasted with bugs that have just three sets of legs. They have two dull hued spots on their bodies that separate them from different vermin. As they suck on the leaves, little yellow spots structure that in the long run combine to give a bronze appearance to the leaves. They likewise produce webbing on the leaf surface as pervasion increments. On the off chance that not controlled when numbers are sensible, they will cause total blanching and passing of the leaves as they suck out every one of the substance of the cells.

Several different parasites exist that additionally harm nursery crops, carmine vermin, and wide bugs. These, in any case, are not generally so common as the two-spotted parasite. They come up short on two dim spots and contrast in shading. The carmine bug is radiant red, while the wide vermin is clear and must be seen with a hand focal point. Expansive parasites cause leaf and natural product deformation.

Thrips: These bugs are particularly drawn to the blossoms. Their particular element is the presence of padded wings. They have grating mouthparts that scratch the leaf surface and suck the plant sap, causing white, brilliant streaks on the leaves. They, similar to whiteflies and aphids, likewise convey infections. Thrips are more drawn to blue tacky traps.

Leafminers: Adult leafminers are flies yellow-dark in shading. They store eggs in the leaves that show as white swellings. As the hatchlings hatch, they eat

"burrows" through the leaf between the upper and lower leaf epidermis, making "mines". As pervasion builds, the mines mix bringing about huge areas of harm that ultimately lead to the passing of the leaf. The full grown hatchlings drop to the ground (surface of the substrate) where they pupate (go through transformation to grown-ups) in 10 days or less. The cycle starts all over again.

Reduce invasions by the evacuation of gravely contaminated leaves and tidy up any fallen leaves from the floor. On the off chance that the substrate is covered with white polyethylene to forestall the hatchlings from entering as they tumble from the leaves, it will limit the multiplication of the bugs. This is especially useful assuming that your plants are filling in pots or beds. The utilization of plastic-wrapped sections will limit the invasion by breaking the life cycle.

Caterpillars and cutworms: These are hatchlings of butterflies and moths, individually. Their presence on crops is demonstrated by scores in leaves and cut stems and leaf petioles. Cutworms move up the plants and feed around evening time, returning to the substrate to stow away during the day. Caterpillars feed constantly. Another indication of their presence is the fertilizers on leaves where they are taking care of. Some hornworms can kill a whole plant in one day or night.
Look for their signs and take them out by hand.
Also, control them by splashing Dipel or Xentari week after week. Dipel and Xentari are a bacterium (Bacillus thuringiensis). This item is extremely protected and is a natural control agent.

Mealybugs: These are famous on peppers, eggplants, and basil. They have an exceptionally trademark appearance of framing a white wax-like substance covering their bodies. It is powder fibers and projections or plates. These fibers shield the bug from contact with many splashes. While utilizing a splash, add a sticker to breakdown the surface pressure of the fibers so the pesticide can contact the bug. There are a couple of useful bugs that go after the pests

Broad vermin: Broad parasites are clear and a lot more modest than the carmine or two-spotted bug. The main indications of harm are the twisting of youthful leaves and their becoming fragile. Not long after the underlying plant answers, the expansive bugs will kill the developing place of the plants. When the developing points
are harmed to the degree that they get and break dry, the plants are lost as they don't effortlessly shape new side shoots. Expansive vermin additionally cause scarring of leafy foods distortion. The natural product isn't useable at that phase of side effect advancement. Luckily, they can be constrained by the utilization of Azatin, Neemix, and Abamectin. A few ruthless vermin keep the expansive parasites in check.

Summary

Keep irritations and infections taken care of in the encompassing region of a lawn nursery. In the event that you are additionally filling in a patio garden in conventional soil throughout the spring and summer, this applies to those harvests as well.
Sanitation in and around the tank-farming framework as referenced before is a decent practice to lessen bothers and diseases.

Finally, keep your plants sound by furnishing them with ideal sustenance and climate. Solid plants have thick fingernail skin and solid tissues that will deter bugs and particularly decrease sicknesses. Stay away from fast vegetative, delicious development of the plants that cause frail development and flimsy tissues that are defenseless to illness disease. While numerous nuisances can harm your yields, their entry to your harvest is more restricted inside than outside in a terrace garden. In any case, when a couple enter they will rapidly increase in the best climate of your crops.

Seek data on large numbers of the supportive sites accessible to recognize and straightaway control the pests.

The great advantage of growing indoors or in a greenhouse is that you can introduce natural biological agents that are predators or parasites of the pests and they will live happily in the environment surrounding the crops keeping the pest population in balance.

In your terrace garden, this regulation of normal specialists is troublesome, on the off chance that certainly feasible, so you should depend more on pesticides.

Use regular pesticides (bioagents), at whatever point fitting rather than synthetic
ones that are tenacious in the plants and climate. With aquaculture, the developing region is at first liberated from all vermin and infections, yet as the yield creates, the entry of such organic entities might happen harming the flying piece of the plants. Watch for them, screen the region with tacky cards, and act rapidly to control them when you experience them. That will make your developing more useful and enjoyable!

MOST COMMON MISTAKES AND HOW TO AVOID THEM

As you start to explore the universe of aquaculture, inspect from these blunders and safeguard them in thought while starting or scaling your framework. Doing so will shop you a ton of sorrow and perchance financial hopelessness related with these seven mistakes.

#1 Mistake

Growers layout unusable or hard-to-use farms

Designing an unusable homestead is a slip-up of inability more noteworthy than whatever else. Numerous producers haven't developed previously (presently not for a huge scope), so they don't contemplate factors like work process and productivity. This outcome in ranches that:

- Don't use house efficiently
- Are difficult to harvest
- Require lots of transplanting and tending
- Aren't conducive to pest control

- Don't allow effortless to get entry to necessary components

Since work is routinely the biggest variable expense on ranches, a work effective configuration is significant. The treatment for this slip-up is to assume cautiously from the start about how you will utilize your system.

Consider your factors as a whole, from developing cravings (light, water, supplements, bothers) to individual longings (access, accommodation, computerization, overt repetitiveness) all along, and exclusively start to arrange your machine when you've basically thought to be these variables.

Talking to mounted producers and voyaging their framework plans can be a very supportive too. Be sure to seek clarification on some pressing issues and situate out what they would do any other way if planning their designs today.

#2 Mistake

Growers underestimate manufacturing and device costs
Most producers starting out in cultivating neglect to totally get their expenses. They begin, put resources into huge offices, expensive utilities, and gear, but not the slightest bit get the danger to completely utilize them on the grounds that the cost range is to eat up through unexpected expenses. A few by and large neglected costs are:

- Packaging
- Pest controls
- Insurance
- Labor
- Printed marketing materials
- Ongoing maintenance
- Heat removal
- Equipment replacement

These are the first expenses that add up. The cardinal sin is that most beginning producers immensely underrate the cost of work whether it's their own or anyone they've recruited. Pontoon fabricating is an occasion of a typical, work concentrated, tank-farming assembling technique.

For pontoon frameworks, the work costs can be huge in general parcel as 45-60 percent of entire expenses. Most makers don't consider this in their work gauges, so when the charge of gathering and handling comes in, the primary concern rapidly drops from the dark to the red.

#3 Mistake

Growers pick out the wrong plants for their local weather or technique

It's helpful to be allured via elegant depictions of extraordinary new yields that populate so many seed indexes nowadays. Assuming I had every dollar returned that I've squandered throughout the years attempting to foster vegetation that is all things considered: a) as of now not pertinent to my creation approach or nearby climate or b) not popular in my local business sectors, I'd have a weighty piece of trade back from seed organizations. Before you pick outcrops, you want to ask a couple questions:

- What constraints are placed on growing utilizing your climate?
- What growing technique will you be using?
- Can you grow this crop with your manufacturing technique?

Different vegetation have stand-out requirements, and some can exclusively be refined in certain ways. People utilizing pontoons have to never again be endeavoring to develop tomatoes. Essentially, individuals with the utilization of beaten rock media need to now not anticipate being skilled to create attractive root crops.

If you live in the Northern Hemisphere, attempting to foster extended day-length crops in an eight-hour day won't turn out pleasantly for you. On the off chance that you're in the south, and continually battling the hotness, attempts to foster a cool-weather conditions crop like rhubarb would be a horrendous decision.

Be insightful about what you grow.

#4 Mistake

Growers grow too big, too fast

Going too immense too fast is a typical mix-up. This leads many laying out cultivators to get financing for enormous, lavish administrations before they catch their expense structure or the market they're endeavoring to support. Cultivators that develop excessively fast likewise appear to have disastrous disappointments extra often.

Big framework disappointment limit monstrous money disappointment; all the more critically, framework disappointment causes an opening in outfit to clients who need consistent conveyance. At the point when this occurs, these clients start to look somewhere else, and via the time the cultivator is returned on the web, he's routinely lost numerous important clients.

These are screw-ups that undermine the total endeavor. Developing gradually, then again, requires persistence, however endorses cultivators to develop into their market naturally, gathering close by needs and needs with items. Enormous contestants will more often than not flood the market with items that they consider are desired
- regularly with consolidated outcomes. There are three things that you can do to avoid the agonies of developing excessively quick: Rein in the craving to overpower the market.

Develop a specialty market.

- Get creative and supply value
- Traversing the mastering curve with grace

Every rancher, whether expert or green, encounters an acquiring information on bend when they begin building out another framework. This much is inescapable. Nonetheless, acquiring information on the bend doesn't need to describe misfortunes and torment. Shrewd arranging is the incredible issue you can accomplish for your ranch, for in spite of the fact that fledgling blunders are unavoidable, huge misfortunes don't need to be.

Ignoring pH levels

The most important estimation for an aquaculture framework is its pH level. Your plants exist, generally, on account of the supplement arrangement. Assuming the arrangement is too acidic or too antacid, your harvests will encounter supplement inadequacies and pass on off.

Get yourself a first rate pH meter and check the pH level somewhere around one time each day. Make a prompt move and bring it back into the equilibrium your plants would blossom with assuming that you notice the pH level sliding in one course or another.

One of the most well-known reasons crops vanish in the aquaculture framework is a messed up pH level. It's difficult to overemphasize how important

checking your pH levels is on the grounds that every one of your yields live in a similar supplement arrangement - every one of your plants would endure assuming your pH is terrible for one plant, as any remaining plants utilize a similar supplement solution.

#6 Mistake

Buying incorrect, cheap or not enough lighting
The right lighting can represent the deciding moment your aqua-farming ranch! Assuming that you purchase close to nothing, your yields will endure. In the event that you purchase some unacceptable sort of lights for your harvests, they will not develop or they'll become hindered. In the event that you pick to purchase the least expensive light you get your hands on, they may not perform and your harvests would die.

Lighting is one of the main speculations you will make as an aquaculture rancher, so go for the best lights for your yield! This calls for complete examination on the sort of light your yields will require on the grounds that various kinds of lights put out various energy types.

Also, don't anticipate that your harvests should consequently flourish since they are set close to a window. That window light is frequently not sufficiently able to help the energetic development you normally anticipate from a tank-farming crop.

#7 Mistake

Using the wrong plant food

There exists the compulsion to just purchase an irregular sack of compost at your nearby nursery place and use it in your tank-farming cultivating framework. All things considered, everything revolves around conveying supplements to the yields, right?

ABSOLUTELY NOT! Regular compost wouldn't weaken totally through your tank-farming framework. Similarly, it will obstruct cylinders and channels. All things being equal, put resources into getting compost planned explicitly for tank-farming cultivating frameworks. Hydroponic fertilizer - available as liquids or granules - meets the growing requirements you require in a soil-light or soil-less garden by providing additional nutrients your crops may otherwise miss if you use the normal fertilizer. There's something else to aqua-farming supplements besides blending great answer for water proportion. Crops developed hydroponically require different N-P-K proportions and different minerals at different places in their development cycle. Whenever crops are in their vegetative development stage they require a ton of nitrogen; while in their blooming stages, they require more phosphorus and potassium.

There are different kinds of aquaculture supplements accessible in the market with various supplement proportions. It is ideal to do some exploration on the harvest you choose to develop to figure out what precisely it requires and at what times to guarantee you are giving your aquaculture garden all that it needs to meet its full potential.

#8 Mistake

Not focusing on sanitation
Don't allow your tank-farming nursery to develop room become a trash canister. Your disinfection propensity meaningfully affects the wellbeing of your yields and for sure your whole tank-farming system.

Without legitimate sterilization, you would spread plant infection starting with one harvest then onto the next and would furnish bothers with appropriate stowing away and taking care of spots.

#9 Mistake

Opting not to learn more

The advanced aquaculture frameworks have been around since the start of the twentieth century and in that time a large number of data and steps directing ranchers has been made accessible. There are huge loads of assets accessible, so regardless of how dark or peculiar an issue you experience may be, there is another person that has encountered it and worked out an answer for it, ask, learn and relearn as advancements come out.

Speak to other aqua-farming ranchers and offer thoughts. The more data you have, the good you will be watching out for your nursery. Generally, you need to furnish your tank-farming nursery with the best and cleanest climate possible.

#10 Mistake

Not enough Oxygen and Improperly Grow-Space

Many novices to aquaculture don't give sufficient oxygen to their harvests underground roots. Crops expect oxygen to be promptly oper. to their underlying foundations for breath likewise with unfortunate root wellbeing comes powerlessness to microbes and infection like root decay. Crops should approach a lot of oxygen, the more the merrier.

Some aquaculture frameworks permit oxygen to the yield's root with only the manner in which they work. A few frameworks, in any case - like profound water culture - would possibly be helped assuming you add more than one air stone. Moreover, guarantee that your nursery has adequate space to develop and in addition to your crops.

#11 Mistake

Not Providing Proper Circulation

With stickiness and warmth, the two of which are generally present in any
aquaculture garden, comes the potential for shape development. To diminish the gamble of shape and comparative issues, you ought to circle the air in the aqua-farming nursery. Adding a fan to your aqua-farming nursery is a basic arrangement that accompanies a few advantages. Assuming your nursery is completely walled it in's, prescribed to add venting that attracts outside air.

On the off chance that you are a fledgling to aqua-farming cultivating, don't neglect the need of legitimate wind stream in your garden.

#12 Mistake

Not Maintaining Temperature

Maintaining great temperatures of both the air and supplement arrangement are frequently disregarded by most amateurs to aqua-farming. How much broke up oxygen present in the supplement arrangements decreases as its temperature climbs. Less oxygen influences root wellbeing and higher temperature is the favored climate for microorganisms, similar to those that cause root decay. Attempt to keep the supplement arrangement between 60-75 degrees. Temperature influences crops in various ways, contingent upon what phase of development it is in. Assuming that the temperature is excessively cold or hot, seeds may not sprout, leafy foods may not frame, and development could slow. Various assortments of harvests additionally have different temperature necessities. For instance, in the event that broccoli or lettuce gets excessively hot, they will bolt. To guarantee the best reap, it is encouraged to explore the ideal developing circumstances for the sort of yields you are looking to grow.

Final Thoughts

As a fledgling to aquaculture, you will undoubtedly commit a few errors and that is essential for learning! Exploring things before time will build your possibilities accomplishing a fruitful tank-farming garden!

BEST HYDROPONIC GARDENING TIPS AND TRICKS

These are the best tips for hydroponics in the garden that I have learned over many years of personal experience (often the hard way). I have seen many people who have tried hydroponics once or twice and have never figured out how to attempt again.

The explanation for the most part can be categorized as one of three categories:

- lack of knowledge- you don't know how things should be or what you need to do
- lack of discipline- you know how things should be, and you know what needs to be done, but you don't take the time or put forth the effort
- lack of ability- you need more first-hand experience, or perhaps you do not have the necessary hydroponic gardening equipment or supplies

All water and supplement arrangements ought to be changed in accordance with pH 6.2 before organization to your plants. The least expensive method for checking your pH is to utilize a pH drop test kit

The tank-farming planting tips am posting underneath will assist you with distinguishing (and cure) your nursery issues. Even after reading such suggestions, it took me two years to make mistakes and learn things the hard way before I changed my approach and took these lessons seriously. As a result, I had the most productive nursery I at any point had. So follow the tips beneath to abbreviate your expectation to learn and adapt by years and obtain incredible outcomes straight away.

The best tips for tank-farming gardening:

• Know what gear you really want and why

• Know the healthful necessities of your plants.

• Know the light/photoperiod prerequisites of your plants

• Use an expert three-section tank-farming supplement product

• Do not utilize extra dietary added substances your first time

• Have a composed dinner plan/plan before you begin

• Have all the vital hardware and supplements before starting

• Garden inside when 55 * F or less outside (or use AC)

• Keep the weight for your lights in an alternate room.

• Check and change your supplement save arrangement each day

• Minimize openness to light to your supplement solution

• Have an extra tank of running water hanging tight for your next supplement change

• Change your water and supplements totally every two weeks.

• Use a computerized clock to control your dim period

• Keep your dull period totally dim and uninterrupted

• Clean and disinfect your framework between crops

• Quarantine new plants for a considerable length of time prior to adding them to your garden

• Do not visit your nursery subsequent to visiting another nursery or being outdoors.

• Do not permit pets in your garden.

• Visit your nursery after a shower and another difference in clothes.

- Have guests to your nursery follow these equivalent rules

- Place a screen or channel over its air bay and outlet (if outdoors)

Have a plan

When requesting as a bundle, the supplements for the most part incorporate printed menus that are not difficult to follow

HydroponiC Gardening's prosperity starts with a strong arrangement. Assuming you have a thought, you want to know your plants' nourishing prerequisites and photoperiod necessities and have the essential supplies and gear to meet those necessities. It would be gainful to have a week by week composed taking care of timetable with dietary qualities and changes. These taking care of directions are consequently produced with General Hydroponics and B.C. starter units, conveyed, nutrient

Food / Nutrients

Don't figure! It is critical to know how intensely you are taking care of your recently established clones, plants, and blossoming plants!

Know the healthful requirements of your plants before you start. Know how powerful the supplements should be consistently in the existence of your plant, and know what the supplements ought to be consistently. Many plants at first need more nitrogen and afterward need more phosphorus to deliver natural product or blossoms. Get a TDS or EC meter so you can follow and change the grouping of the supplement arrangement as your plants grow.

Nutrients have generally given me extraordinary outcomes and require negligible pH revision contrasted with other nutrients.

Don't attempt to blend your vegetables. All things being equal, begin with an expert tank-farming supplement item. These are typically three-section frameworks that are exhaustive (and simple to utilize). My most loved is BC Nutrients from Technaflora. When your aquaculture cultivating framework is functional and obtain incredible outcomes, you can have a go at blending your extraordinary plant food sources assuming that you need. To some degree then you know precisely where the issue is when things don't work!

B1 is continuously driving cell division and plant development. I use it in each drop of water from start to finish.

Similar applies to the utilization of supplement added substances. Try not to attempt to work on the exhibition with the option of a great deal of extra material to your supplement supply (basically not from the outset). This is one of the tips for tank-farming in the nursery that I wind up rehashing to everybody I help! To start with, feed just the three-section vital supplements until your aqua-farming nursery framework works without a hitch and accomplishes magnificent outcomes. Assuming you need, you can have a go at adding vitamin B1, fluid green growth, or silica (or all three).

An extra supplement repository helps a great deal with regards to making a total supplement arrangement. The pack here is heavy!

You will test and protect your inventory of supplements consistently, all things considered. Following fourteen days of utilizing similar supplements, you can go on with new water and new supplements once more. The best method for doing this is to give two tanks of supplements, one with a supplement answer for your aquaculture cultivating strategy and one with water for your next difference in nutrients.

I can't pressure how significant this aqua-farming nursery tip is! The subsequent tank permits the water to dechlorinate and arrive at room temperature, safeguarding its foundations. See additionally my page on aquaculture nutrients.

Root Health

Healthy roots are for the most part white; 16-ounce individual cups are modest lattice pots

If the roots are harmed, they can't assimilate supplements to take care of the plants. Harm underground prompts soil harm like dead leaves and unhealthy plants. Safeguard your foundations by appropriately focusing on your supplement arrangement, utilizing two tank-farming supplement repositories (one with running water for your next supplement change), and limiting how much light that interacts with your supplement arrangement. This forestalls green growth that forestall parasitic mosquitoes and forestall most root harm problems.

Adequate Lighting

A 600 watt light is great for a nursery estimating 4 x 4 to 4 x 8 inches

There are not many easy routes with regards to lighting an indoor nursery. You really want no less than 40 watts/square foot, however 60 watts/square foot. It would be better. Most high-pressure incandescent lights work effectively and are the most well known choices. For different reasons, I suggest a 600 watt light or a 1000 watt light. On the off chance that you really want assistance picking a light, attempt my light choice device. This is one of your most massive costs: Expect to pay a normal of $ 400 to $ 600 for a good framework (light + reflector + ballast).

The T5 fluorescent lights are ideally suited for clones and the vegetable region. A more sturdy light is generally wanted in the blossom area

Some tips for aquaculture in the nursery of fluorescent lights: Regular fluorescent lights don't transmit sufficient usable light for sound development and are just reasonable for clones, seedlings or exceptionally youthful plants in the vegetative stage (spinach, lettuce, culinary spices). In the event that you decide to involve bright lights in your developing space, T5 lights (otherwise called Tek lights) are the main choice. While T5 lights produce less hotness than HID lights, they just produce about a large portion of a watt for every watt. You likewise need to keep the tips of your plants a couple creeps from the light, which at times turns into a genuine aggravation in the butt.

Controlling the Temperature

With an advanced indoor/outside thermometer, you can screen the temperature in the development room AND the temperature at its problem area (straightforwardly under the light).

One of the greatest tips for aquaculture in the nursery is temperature control! Plant development stops rapidly when the temperature increases over 85 degrees (except if you are persistently siphoning CO_2). The HID developing lights radiate a great deal of hotness, which makes temperature control a major issue for the indoor nursery. Setting the weight for your light outside of the development room helps (provided that you have an old balance for solenoids and no new computerized stabilizer), however even that isn't sufficient. Radial fans or enclosure fans are an outright should (see the design of the exhaust air fan). As far as I can tell, fans alone are sufficiently not. What is required is a chilly/cool air source.

Centrifugal fans are the most effective air engines, whether you inhale hot air or suck in new, cool air.

After long stretches of biological and aqua-farming cultivation, I thought of only two hints for the aquaculture nursery to take care of this issue. Anticipate developing inside as long as the external temperature is 55F or less. This permits you to draw new, dry air (from an outside source) into your nursery as it extinguishes the hot air. The main other choice is to siphon the air conditioner!

Photoperiod Manipulation

Growing tents is a fast method for setting up a light-close nursery region. The enormous tents offer adequate room so that fans and, surprisingly, an island can keep up with the garden.

Many plants need more limited times of sunlight to set off blooming/fruiting. The following are two hints for the outcome of aquaculture cultivating: First, the lights ought to be switched now and again simultaneously every day (utilize an advanced timer!).

Deluxe Version - Better endlessly vents, and somewhat more space for a regular 8 x 8 x 6-foot garden

Second, plants should be kept in outright, complete obscurity hindered by the UN during the dull period. Utilize a totally obscured space for the nursery or an obscured tent. Plants can be defenseless to them, so don't attempt to stay away from them! For more data, see my page on constraining flowers.

The Right Equipment/Tools

A computerized clock is valuable for controlling lights, humidifiers, and fans. As I would like to think, it is critical for a fruitful blossoming room!

Do not begin your nursery until you have totally covered the base regions as a whole. You want a totally dull region, an elite presentation fan, adequate light, a tank-farming nursery framework, aquaculture supplements, a swaying fan, a TDS meter (or EC meter), a pH test unit, and potentially an air conditioner.

CONCLUSION

Hydroponic indoor nurseries develop like some other indoor nursery with artificial

lighting. The distinction between indoor nursery developing and aquaculture developing is on the grounds that you don't utilize any soil.

An in-line siphon then, at that point, circles supplement advanced water through the plant's underground root growth, while upward lighting permits plants to finish the ordinary photosynthesis cycle they need to grow.

Inert development media gives you the opportunity and control to make how much compost the plant gets substantially more refined and furnishes the roots with considerably more oxygen.

Maybe you are as of now a grounds-keeper and you're interested about soilless development or tank-farming and how it is ideal. Aquaculture cultivating, under completely controlled conditions, is an ideal method for developing vegetables, organic products, and herbs.

Here is a rundown of certain reasons why.

1. Space-saving

Hydroponics saves an incredible measure of room contrasted with customary soil nurseries. As a general rule, the foundations of a plant need space to spread in the dirt. That's it! All things being equal, they are submerged in a shower with oxygenated supplement solution.

Imagine having all that you really want to eat in a little pill.

You don't need to search for food or eat three dinners every day - you just took the pill, and your body got an ideal portion of nutrients.

This is what aquaculture offers your plants. Rather than involving the dirt as need might arise, tank-farming purposes a redid supplement answer for encompass your plants with impeccably aligned nourishment consistently. Plants don't need to spread their foundations like in the ground for supplements, and that implies more modest root systems.

For this explanation, you can pack your plants nearer together, which prompts colossal space savings.

It has been referenced that tank-farming developing expects up to half less land to grow.

2. More efficient use of water

When a landscaper watering plants in the traditional soil garden, a portion of the water dribbles from the lower part of his holder or keeps on spilling into the dirt. Some portion of it vanishes from the beginning. The plant requires just a small level of the atmosphere.

Hydroponics tackles the issue of inundating agricultural waste in the dirt by utilizing a supposed recycling supplement repository in many frameworks (profound water culture is one of the most popular).

This implies that the foundations of a plant retain just the necessary measure of water whenever and leave the rest in the tank for some other time. The tank is covered to forestall dissipation, and no water can escape from the floor.

It makes a similar measure of water utilized for watering a plant in the ground for a day, to water a plant in an aquaculture climate for days or weeks. Around 90% of the water utilized can be put something aside for cultivating by just changing to a tank-farming environment.

3. Faster and greater potential yields
Hydroponics speeds up plant development 30% quicker than in the dirt. Hydroponically developed plants will quite often develop much faster and more broad than customarily developed soil plants. The primary justification for why plants can fill quicker in a tank-farming framework is that cultivators can deliver the best mix of supplements. This is conveyed straightforwardly to the plant's root foundations through a nonstop progression of supplement arrangement. Since these supplements are consumed straight by the roots, plants don't have to utilize energy to look for supplements, as would be the situation in the dirt where plant food sources are weakened. Therefore, the root foundations in aquaculture plants don't develop, so this development presently appears as up growth.

If you develop outside, quicker development implies you can get more harvest cycles before your it is over to develop season. For instance, in tank-farming, you can get lettuce from seedling to reap about a month contrasted with two months in soil.

More plants can fill in an aqua-farming nursery simultaneously. This is on the grounds that their root foundations are not battling for the space expected to track down an adequate number of supplements, as would be the situation in the dirt. An even dissemination of the

supplement arrangement makes rivalry superfluous, and that implies that the maker can present plants with a higher thickness into the system.

Hydroponic development implies that you can grow up to 80% more natural products, buds, and flowers.

4. Cleaner, soil-less, so less chaos

Most aquaculture cultivating is done inside or in nurseries. Tank-farming is normally unlimited. This implies that it doesn't need to get excessively grimy as in a customary garden.

5. Can be grown almost anywhere

As NASA space travelers get ready to satisfy the vision of room investigation with progressively lengthy missions, researchers are attempting to figure out how to develop their food. Tank-farming fits impeccably on the grounds that plants can be developed upward under controlled soilless circumstances and in more modest rooms. Aquaculture is ideal for individuals who need plants and vegetables to develop yet have restricted space or land. Develop on Walls, gallery in your deck, in your level, on Mars, in the Arctic Circle, on a ship!

6. Fewer pests and diseases - fewer pesticides

Most plant-causing bugs and microorganisms happen in the dirt. The dirt is taken out from the image and supplanted with one of the typical aqua-farming development media. Soil evacuation additionally takes out a significant number of the different soil-borne illnesses and nuisances that plague conventional planting. On the off chance that plants are filled in controlled indoor spaces and are sound, irritations and illnesses are substantially less normal. Cleaning can make a huge commitment to keeping away from likely issues. No root decay, less perilous contagious disease

7. It can be done all year round.

Most of the tank-farming development happens in nurseries or even inside. Assuming you develop inside under controlled conditions, you have some control over temperature and light, as well as supplements, and that implies it doesn't rely upon occasional and outer changes. Inside or outside, your plants are safeguarded from downpour, hail, slush, snow, storms, and windstorms from Mars.

8. Easier to harvest

Many aqua-farming frameworks can be planned considering harvest. Not at all like a field where the specialist needs to twist and work with the ground ceaselessly, an aquaculture framework can be intended to be in a more ideal vertical position. For instance, strawberries can be developed over the ground, and the ready natural products hang down for simple reaping. The tank-farming framework can be adjusted whenever for better ergonomics and productivity.

9. Full control

Hydroponics can be estimated more precisely than conventional cultivating, and numerous gadgets can be utilized for this reason. There is a wide range of PH monitors and conductivity meters that you can use to monitor your nutrients and even a system that can automatically dose the tank to the designated areas.

10. No weeding - less work

Except for a media-filled sheet material framework, there might be basically no possibility for weeds that poor person been purposely planted. Without soil, without weeds. No weeding to crush your spirit. Weeds don't fill in tank-farming. Thusly, you have seen the reason why this book is opportune for you. Tank-farming planting is something that you ought to check out today.

Good luck with it!

9 798802 391860